T. N. Burke

**Ireland's Case Stated in Reply to Mr. Froude**

T. N. Burke

**Ireland's Case Stated in Reply to Mr. Froude**

ISBN/EAN: 9783744715782

Printed in Europe, USA, Canada, Australia, Japan

Cover: Foto ©ninafisch / pixelio.de

More available books at **www.hansebooks.com**

# IRELAND'S CASE STATED

IN REPLY TO

## MR. FROUDE.

BY THE

## VERY REV. T. N. BURKE, O.P.

"*Nec tecum possum vivere nec sine te.*"

NEW YORK:
P. J. KENEDY,
EXCELSIOR CATHOLIC PUBLISHING HOUSE,
5 BARCLAY STREET.
1883.

Entered according to act of Congress, in the year 1872, by
P. M. HAVERTY,
In the Office of the Librarian of Congress at Washington.

*Imprimatur*

F<sup>R</sup>. M. D. LILLY, O.P.

F. I. R. MEAGHER, O.P.

---
LANGE, LITTLE & HILLMAN,
PRINTERS, ELECTROTYPERS AND STEREOTYPERS,
108 TO 114 WOOSTER STREET, N. Y.
---

# PREFACE.

WHEN I was first asked to reply to Mr. Froude's lectures, I was very unwilling to do it. As a priest, I felt reluctant to enter upon a controversy which promised to be purely secular. As an Irishman, I thought that Mr. Froude's was only one other utterance of those old anti-Irish calumnies which it has been the fashion of English writers to invent and repeat, and which have been discussed, answered, refuted a hundred times. My friends, however, urged their request, and Mr. Froude's lectures took a tone so damaging at once to the Irish character, and so bitterly hostile to the Catholic religion, that I felt justified in attempting to answer him in defense of my faith and my country.

I cannot claim for my lectures anything like completeness as an answer to Mr. Froude. The call upon me was so sudden, and the time so short; the ground which Mr. Froude covered was so extensive, and the means of meeting him—such as authorities, references, etc.—so limited on my part, that I am far from satisfied with my work, and I have heard with pleasure that **Mr. John Mitchel, whose** great historical knowledge, vigorous style, and undoubted love for Ireland, render him eminently fitted for the task, has undertaken in a series of papers to meet and refute the views of the English historian. The warmth of debate led Mr. Froude, in his rejoinder to **me, not only** into a temporary forgetfulness of the usual courtesies of gentlemen, but also **into** assertions which have been repudiated and disproved; such **for** example as making the Catholic Church **answerable for the bloody** edicts of Charles **the Fifth, a** monarch who never hesitated to persecute **the Church and her head whenever** policies dictated, **who** coquetted with **the reformers of** the Reformation, **until** policy dictated **an opposite** course, and whose army committed more terrible ravages on Rome, than any that we read of—Goth, Vandal, or Lombard.

The Church, **however,** that for nineteen hundred years has withstood and conquered every opponent, **is** not likely to **fall** before **the** small, though poisoned spear of a **Froude;** and the Irish nationality, which has survived **all** the efforts **of** England and all the calumnies of **her** writers for **seven hundred years, is not likely to** be withered **up by the scorn, nor** made effete by the sneering sympathy **of such a man as** he **who now** stands before **the American** world, pitying, reviling, scorning the **Irish** people **and** their history.

# CONTENTS.

### LECTURE I.
THE NORMAN INVASION, . . . . 9

### LECTURE II.
IRELAND UNDER THE TUDORS, . 59

### LECTURE III.
IRELAND UNDER CROMWELL, . . . 96

### LECTURE IV.
GRATTAN AND THE VOLUNTEERS, . . 152

### LECTURE V.
IRELAND SINCE THE UNION, . . . 199
APPENDIX, . . . . . . 229

# LECTURE I.

# THE NORMAN INVASION.

LADIES AND GENTLEMEN: It is a strange fact that the old battle that has been raging for seven hundred years, should be renewed again so far away from the old land. The question on which I am come to speak to you this evening has been argued at many a council board, debated in many a Parliament, disputed on many a well-fought field, and is not yet decided—the question between England and Ireland. Amongst the visitors to America, who came over this year, there was one gentleman, distinguished in Europe for his style of writing and for his historical knowledge, the author of several works which have created a profound sensation, at least for their originality. Mr. Froude has frankly stated that he came over to this country to deal with England and with the Irish question, viewing it from an English standpoint; that like a true man he came to America to make the best case that he could for his own country; that he came to state that case to an American public as to a grand jury, and to demand a verdict from them, the most extraordinary that was ever yet demanded from any people, namely, the declaration that England was right in the manner in which she has treated my native land for seven hundred years.[1] It seems, according to this learned gentleman, that we Irish have been badly treated—so much he confesses; but he puts in as a plea that we only got what we deserved. It is true, he says, that we have governed them badly; the reason is, because it was impossible to govern them rightly. It is true that we have robbed them; the reason is, because it was a pity to leave them their own, they made such a bad use of it. It is true we have persecuted them; the reason is, persecution was a fashion of the time, and the order of the day. On these pleas there is not a criminal in prison to-day in the United States that should not instantly get his freedom by acknowledging his crime and pleading some extenuating circumstance. Our ideas about Ireland have been all wrong, it seems. Seven hundred years ago the exigencies of the time demanded the foundation of a strong British Empire; in order to do this, Ireland had to be conquered, and Ireland was conquered. Since that time the one ruling idea in the English mind has been to do all the good that they could for the Irish. Their legislation and their action has not always been tender, but it has been always beneficent. They sometimes were severe, but they were severe to us for our own good; and the difficulty of England has been that the Irish, during these long hundreds of years, never understood their own interests, or knew what was for their own advantage. Now, the American mind is enlightened, and henceforth no Irishman must complain of the past, in this new light in which Mr. Froude puts it before us. Now, the amiable gentleman tells us that what has been our fate in the past, he greatly fears we must reconcile ourselves to in the future. He comes to tells us his version of the history of Ireland, and he also comes to solve Ireland's difficulty, and to lead us out of all the miseries that have been our lot for hundreds of years. When he came many persons questioned what was the motive or the reason of his coming? I have heard people speaking all around me, and assigning to the learned gentleman this motive or that. Some people said he was an emissary of the English Government; that they sent him here because they were beginning to be afraid of the rising power of Ireland in this great nation; that they saw here eight millions of Irishmen by birth, and perhaps fourteen millions by descent; and that they knew enough of the Irish to realize that the Almighty God blessed them always with an extraordinary power, not only to preserve themselves, but to spread themselves, until, in a few years, not fourteen, but fifty millions of descendants of Irish blood and of Irish race will be in this land." According to those who thus surmise, England wants to check the sympathy of the American people for their Irish fellow-citizens, and it was considered that the best way to effect this was to send a learned man with a plausible story to this country—a man with a singular power of viewing facts in the light in which he wishes to view them and put them before others; a man with the extraordinary faculty of so mixing up these facts, that many simple-minded people will look upon them, as he puts them before them, as true, and whose mission it was to alienate the mind of America from Ireland to-day, by showing what an impracticable, obstinate, accursed race we are.

Others, again, surmised that the learned gentleman came for another purpose; they said: "England is in the hour of her weakness; she is tottering fast and visibly to her ruin; the disruption of that old empire is evidently approaching; she is to-day cut off, without an ally in Europe. Her army a cipher; her fleet—according to Mr. Reade, a great authority on this question—nothing to be compared to the rival fleet of the great Russian power now growing up. When France was paralyzed by her late defeat, England lost her best ally. The three emperors, in their meeting the other day, contemptuously ignored her, and they settled the affairs of the world, without as much as mentioning the name of that kingdom which was once so powerful. Her resources of coal and iron are failing; her people are discontented, and she is showing every sign of decay."[1] Thus did some people argue that England was anxious for an American alliance, for they said, "What would be more natural than that the old, tottering empire should seek to lean on the strong, mighty, vigorous young arm of America?" and Mr. Froude's mission, according to these persons, seemed intended to prepare the way for such alliance.

I have heard others say that the gentleman came over to this country on the invitation of a little clique of sectarian bigots. Men who, feeling that the night of religious bigotry and sectarian bitterness is fast coming to a close before the increasing light of American intelligence and education, would fain prolong the darkness for an hour or two, by whatever help Mr. Froude could lend them.

But I protest to you, gentlemen, here to-night, that I have heard all these motives assigned to this learned man, without giving them the least attention. I believe Mr. Froude's motives to be simple, straightforward, honorable, and patriotic. I am willing to give him credit for the highest motives, and I consider him perfectly incapable of lending himself to any base or sordid proceedings, from a base or sordid motive. But, as the learned gentleman's motives have been so freely canvassed and criticised—and I believe, indeed, in many cases, misinterpreted—so my own motives in coming here to-night may be perhaps also misinterpreted and misunderstood, unless I state them clearly and plainly. As he has been said to come as an emissary of the English Government, so I may be said, perhaps, to appear as an emissary of rebellion and revolution. As he is supposed by some to have the sinister motive of alienating the American mind from the Irish citizenship of the States, so I may be suspected of endeavoring to excite religious or political hatred. Now, I protest these are not my motives. I come here to-night simply to defend the honor of Ireland in her history. I come here to-night lest any man should think that in this our day, or in any day, Ireland is to be left without a son who will speak for the mother that bore him.

And, first of all, I hold that Mr. Froude is unfit for the task that he has undertaken, for three great reasons. First, because I find in the writings of this learned gentleman that he has solemnly and emphatically declared that he despairs of ever finding a remedy for Ireland, and he gives it up as a bad job. Here are his words, written in one of his essays a few years ago: "The present hope," he says, "is that by assiduous justice, that is, by conceding everything that the Irish please to ask, we shall disarm that enmity and convince them of our good will. It may be so. There are persons sanguine enough to hope that the Irish will be so moderate in what they demand, and the English so liberal in what they will grant, that at last we shall fling ourselves into each other's arms in tears of mutual forgiveness. I do not share that expectation. It is more likely that they will press their importunities till we turn upon them and refuse to yield further. There will be a struggle once more, and either the emigration to America will increase in volume till it has carried the entire race beyond our reach, or in some shape or other they will again have to be coerced into submission."

Banish them or coerce them! There is the true Englishman speaking. My only remedy, he emphatically says, my only hope, my only prospect of a future for Ireland is, let them go to America; have done with the race altogether, and give us an Ireland at last such as we have labored to make it for seven hundred years, a desert and a solitude. Or, if they remain at home they will have to be coerced into submission. I hold that this gentleman has no right to come to America to tell the American people and the Irish in America that he can cast the horoscope of Ireland's future. He has acknowledged his inability and unfitness for this task in the words I have just quoted.

The original sin of the Englishman in his dealings with the Irish people and their history is his contempt of them. The average Englishman despises the Irishman, looks down upon him as a being almost inferior in nature. This feeling may not be expressed, but it lies deep though dormant in the hearts of most Englishmen, even though they be unconscious of its existence.' I make no distinction of English, Catholic or Protestant. I speak from the experience of intercourse, and I believe the feeling to be common to all. I know many Englishmen, amiable, generous, charming characters, who would not cherish such a feeling consciously, nor express it for the whole world; yet I have seen it come forth from them in a thousand forms, as if it were their very nature. I mention this not to excite animosity or to create bad blood or bitter feeling; no. I protest this is not my meaning; but I mention this because I am convinced it lies at the very root of this antipathy and of that hatred between the English and Irish, which seems to be incurable; and I verily believe that until that feeling is destroyed, you never can have cordial union between these two countries; and the only way to destroy it is by raising Ireland, through justice and by home legislation, that she may attain such a position that she will enforce and command the respect of her English fellow-subjects. Mr. Froude, himself, who, I am sure, is incapable of any ungenerous sentiment towards any man or any people, is an actual living example of that feeling of contempt of which I speak. In November, 1856, this learned gentleman addressed a Scottish assembly in Edinburgh; the subject of his address was, "The Influence of the Reformation on the Scottish Character." According to him, it made the Scotch the finest people on the face of the earth. Originally fine, they never got their last touch—that made them as it were, archangels amongst men—until the holy hand of John Knox was laid upon them. On that occasion the learned gentleman introduced himself to his Scottish audience in the following words: "I have undertaken," he says, "to speak this evening on the effects of the Reformation in Scotland, and I consider myself a very bold person to have come here on any such undertaking; in the first place, the subject is one with which it is presumptuous for a stranger to meddle. Great national movements can only be understood properly by the people whose disposition they represent. We say ourselves about our own history, that Englishmen only can properly comprehend it. It is the same with every considerable nation. They work out their own political and spiritual lives through tempers, humors, and passions peculiar to themselves, and the same disposition which produces the result is required to interpret it afterwards." Did the learned gentleman offer any such apology for entering so boldly upon the discussion of Irish affairs? Oh no; there was no apology necessary; he was only going to speak of the "mere Irish." There was no word to express his own fear that perhaps he did not understand the Irish character, or the subject upon which he was about to treat; there was no apology to the Irish in America—the supposed fourteen millions—when he so boldly takes up their history, endeavoring to hold them up as a licentious, immoral, irreligious, contentious, obstinate, unmanageable race; not at all. It was not necessary; they were only Irish. If they were Scotch, then the learned gentleman would have come with a thousand apologies for his own presumption in venturing to approach such a delicate subject as the delineation of the Scottish character, or anything connected with it.

What, on the other hand, is his treatment of the Irish? I have, in this book before me, words that came from his pen, and I protest as I read them I felt every drop of my blood boil in my veins. He compares us, in this essay, to a pack of hounds. He virtually says: "To deliver Ireland, to give Ireland any meed of freedom, would be the same as when a gentleman, addressing his hounds, said, 'I give you your freedom; now go out to act for yourselves.'" The pack, it is needless to say, after worrying all the sheep in the neighborhood, ended by tearing each other to pieces.

Now, we Irish are naturally a proud people. The antiquity of our race, the purity of our blood, preserved through the ancient form of government by clans or families, the fact that serfdom never existed in any form in Ireland, the consciousness of intellectual gifts and power, the strange imaginativeness with which we are endowed, our romantic, though unfortunate history, so full of disaster yet so full of glory; all these, and other causes, have made us perhaps the proudest people on the earth. Now, we all know that a proud people are only made the more sensitive by misfortune, and that they will brook actual injury and accept the fiercest hatred rather than submit to be despised or treated with contempt. This strong natural pride of the Irish has never been considered for a moment by England's statesmen in dealing with the Irish people, nor by her writers in describing them. And yet, there it lies, deeply seated in the Irish character, and the man who ignores it will never be able to understand the philosophy of Irish history.

But if the learned historian be so far unfitted by his nationality for dealing with Irish subjects, still more is he rendered unfit for this work by his religious views and opinions. Every calm and unprejudiced mind that studies the history of Ireland must at once perceive that this people's Catholic faith and religion has been for the last three hundred years the mainspring of their national life and action. Ireland's Catholicity has been the source of her bitterest sorrows and highest joys. The Catholic faith may have sat lightly on other peoples—in Ireland it entered into the very heart and soul of the nation. Elsewhere it may have been an intellectual conviction—in Ireland it was an absorbing passion. In other lands we may regard it as a hallowed tradition—in Ireland it was a personal as well as national divine power and influence, before which all other considerations were to yield, to which all interests, even life itself, were to be sacrificed. First in the nation's heart and love, the Catholic faith was our all in all. That man alone can understand the feelings, the genius, the character, the history of Ireland and of her people, who knows, values, and appreciates this religion of theirs; who understands the strong hold which it can take of a man or a people, and the extraordinary power with which it can shape character, influence policy, and determine the color and the purposes of life.

Now, how does Mr. Froude view this great and mighty secret of Irish life and action? He dismisses the subject with a few contemptuous words. He says it is "a matter of which one knows as much as another, and all of us know nothing."

It is not, however, contempt only he feels for Ireland's religion; it is the deepest detestation and hatred.* In his mind the Catholic Church and religion is associated with all that is most monstrous and vile, and when he comes to treat of anything or any people connected with that religion he is unreliable—no longer to be trusted. He cannot speak the truth, because he can no longer see it. He is blind, not only in mental perception, but even in conscience. He no longer hesitates to say and do things which all men pronounce unfair, dishonorable, and insulting to our common sense. The very gentlemen who rallied round him and received him in New York, told him plainly enough how little they relied on his word as an historian, whenever he had a cause to plead or a special theory to work out. He undertook to vindicate Queen Elizabeth and to blacken Mary, Queen of Scots. In doing this he has been convicted of what surely is a crime in any one pretending to write history, namely, giving his own conclusions and words as if they were quotations from ancient historians or authentic records. Mr. Froude, writes Mr. Meline, has never grasped the meaning of inverted commas.

His hero is Henry VIII., and in order to justify this monster, he converts his known vices into virtues, his rapacity is only zeal for pure doctrine, his lust a chaste anxiety for the public good. One or two facts as related by him will settle the question of his veracity as an historian.

One fact will show you how this gentleman treats history. When King Henry VIII. declared war against the Church, and when all England was convulsed by his tyranny—one day hanging a Catholic because he would not deny the supremacy of the Pope, the next day hanging a Protestant because he denied the Real Presence—anybody that differed from Henry was sure to be sent to the scaffold. It was a sure and expeditious way of silencing all argument.

During this time, when the monasteries were beginning to be pillaged, the Catholic clergy of England, especially those who remained faithful to the Pope, were most odious to the tyrant; and such was the slavish acquiescence of the English people that they began to hate their clergy in order to please their king. Well, at this time, a certain man whose name was Hunn was lodged a prisoner in the Tower, and was found hanged by the neck in his cell. There was a coroner's inquest held upon him, and the twelve ruffians—I can call them nothing else—in order to express their hatred for the Church, and to please the powers that were, found a verdict against the chancellor of the Bishop of London, a most excellent priest, whom everybody knew to be such. When the bishop heard of this verdict, he applied to the prime minister to have the verdict quashed. He brought the matter before the House of Lords, in order that the character of his chancellor might be fully vindicated. The king's attorney-general took cognizance of it by a solemn decree, and the verdict of the coroner's inquest was set aside, and the twelve men declared to be twelve perjurers. Now, listen to Mr. Froude's version of that story. He says: The clergy of the time were reduced to such a dreadful state that actually a coroner's inquest returned a verdict of willful murder against the chancellor of the Bishop of London, and the bishop was obliged to apply to Cardinal Wolsey to have a special jury to try him; because, if he took any ordinary jury in London, they would have found him guilty—leaving the reader under the impression that this priest, this chancellor, was a monster of iniquity, and the priests of the time were as bad as he; leaving the impression that this man was guilty of the murder, who was as innocent as Abel, and hinting that, if put on trial before twelve of his countrymen, they would have found him guilty on the evidence. This is the version he puts upon it—he knowing the facts as well as I know them.

This, then, is the manner of man with whom we have to deal. He comes to ask America to indorse by her verdict England's treatment of Ireland. He acknowledges that England found us free, and enslaved us, and he asks the people of America to say before the world that England was right. He confesses that the land of Ireland was by right and just title the property and possession of the Celt, and that England robbed us of that land by war and spoliation, and he asks the American people to proclaim that England was right. He tells us that the people of Ireland were devotedly Catholic, and that England, by every unjust and cruel means, persecuted that people for their religious convictions for over two hundred years, and he calls upon the great land of civil and religious freedom to approve of England's persecution.'

Well, now, my friends, we come to consider the subject of his first lecture. Indeed, I must say I never practically experienced the difficulty of hunting a will-o'-the-wisp in a marsh, until I came to follow this learned gentleman in his first lecture. I say nothing disrespectful of him at all, but simply say, he covered so much ground, at such unequal distances, that it was next to impossible to follow him. He began by remarking how General Rufus King wrote a letter about certain Irishmen, and he says that the Catholics of Ireland sympathized with England, while the Protestants of Ireland were breast-high for America, in the old struggle between this country and Great Britain. All these questions which belong to our day, I will leave aside for the close of these lectures. When I come to speak of the men and things of our own day, then I shall have great pleasure in taking up Mr. Froude's assertions. But, coming home to the great question of Ireland, what does this gentleman tell us? Seven hundred years ago Ireland was invaded by the Anglo-Normans. The first thing, apparently, that he wishes to do, is to justify this invasion, and establish the principle that the Normans were right in coming to Ireland. He began by drawing a terrible picture of the state of Ireland before the invasion: They were cutting each other's throats; the whole land was covered with bloodshed; there was in Ireland neither religion, morality, or government; therefore the Pope found it necessary to send the Normans to Ireland, as you would send a policeman into a saloon where the people were killing one another. This is his justification—that in Ireland, seven hundred years ago, just before the Norman invasion, there was neither religion, morality, or government. Let us see if he is right?

The first proof that he gives that there was no government in Ireland is a most insidious statement. He says: How could there be any government in a country where every family maintained itself according to its own ideas of right or wrong, acknowledging no authority. Now, if this be true, in one sense of the word family, certainly Ireland was in a most deplorable state. Every family governing itself according to its own notions, and acknowledging no authority! What does he mean by the words every family? Speaking to Americans in the nineteenth century, it means every household in the land. We speak of a family as composed of father, mother, and three or four children gathered around the domestic hearth; this is our idea of the family. I freely admit if in this sense every family in Ireland were governed by their own ideas—admitting of no authority over them— he has established his case in one thing against Ireland. But what is the meaning of the words every family? Irishmen who hear me to-night know it meant the sept or tribe that had the same name. They owned two or three counties and a large extent of territory. Men of the same name were called the men of the same family. The MacMurraghs, of Leinster; the O'Tooles, of Wicklow; the O'Byrnes, of Kildare; the O'Connors, of Connaught; the O'Neills and the O'Donnells, of Ulster. The "family" meant a nation. Two or three counties were governed by one chieftain, and represented by one man of the sept. It is quite true that each family governed itself in its own independence, and acknowledged no superior. There were five great families in Ireland: the O'Connors, in Connaught; the O'Neills, in Ulster; the MacLoughlins, in Meath; the O'Briens, in Munster; and the MacMurraghs, in Leinster. And under these five great heads there were minor septs and smaller families, each counting from five or six hundred to perhaps a thousand fighting men, but all acknowledging in the different provinces their sovereignty to these five great royal houses. These five houses again elected their monarch, or supreme ruler, called the Ardrigh, who dwelt in Tara. Now, I ask you if "family" meant the whole sept, or tribe, or army in the field defending their rights and liberties, having a regularly constituted authority and head, is it fair to say that the country was in anarchy because every family governed themselves according to their own notions? Is it fair for this gentleman to try to hoodwink and deceive the American jury to which he has made his appeal, by describing the Irish "family," which meant a sept or tribe, as a family of the nineteenth century, which means only the head of the house, with the mother and the children?

Again he says: In this deplorable state the people lived, like the New-Zealanders of to-day live, in underground caves. And then he boldly says: That I myself opened up in Ireland one of these underground lodging-houses. Now, mark. This gentleman lived in Ireland a few years ago; and he discovered a rath in Kerry. In it he found some remains of mussel-shells and bones. At the time of the discovery he had the most learned archæologist in Ireland with him, and they put their heads together about it. Mr. Froude has written in this very book that "what these places were intended for, or the uses they were applied to, baffled all conjecture; no one could tell." Then, if it baffled all conjecture, and he did not know what to make of it—if it so puzzled him then that nobody could declare what they were for, what right has he to come out to America and say they were the ordinary dwellings of the Irish people?

In order to understand the Norman invasion, I must ask you to consider, first, my friends, the ancient Irish Constitution which governed the land. Ireland was governed by septs or families. The land, from time immemorial, was in the possession of these families or tribes. Each tribe elected its own chieftain, and to him they paid the most devoted obedience and allegiance, so that the fidelity of the Irish clansman to his chief was proverbial. The mutual independence of the septs or tribes was founded on what is known to-day in America as the democratic principle of State Rights. The chief, during his lifetime, convoked an assembly of the tribe again, and they elected from among the princes of his family the best and the strongest man to be his successor, and they called him the Tanist. The object of this was that the successor of the king might be known, and that, at the king's or the prince's death, there might be no riot or bloodshed, or contention for the right of succession to him. Was this not a wise law? The elective monarchy has its advantages. The best man comes to the front, because he is the choice of his fellow-men. For when they come to elect a successor to their prince, they choose the best man. Not of necessity the king's eldest son, who might be a booby or a fool.

And so they came together and wisely selected the best, the strongest, the bravest, and the wisest man, and he was acknowledged to have the right to the succession. He was the Tanist, according to the ancient law of Ireland. Well, these families, as we said, in the various provinces of Ireland, owed allegiance and paid it to the king of the province. He was one of the five great families called in after ages the "five bloods." Each prince had his own judge or Brehon, who administered justice in the court to the people. These Brehons, or judges, were learned men; the historians of the time tell us that they could speak Latin as fluently as they could speak Irish; they had established a code of law, and in their colleges studied that law, and when they had graduated in their studies, they came home to their respective septs or tribes, and were established as judges or Brehons over the people. Nay, more! Nowhere in the history of the Irish do we hear of an instance where a man rebelled or protested against the decision of his Brehon judge. Then these five monarchs in the provinces elected an Ardrigh, or high king. With him they sat in council on national matters within the halls of imperial Tara.

There Patrick found them in the year 432, minstrels, and bards, and Brehons, princes, crowned monarchs, and high king; there did he find them discussing, like lords and true men, the affairs of the nation, when he preached to them the faith of Jesus Christ. And, while this Constitution remained, the clansmen paid no rent for their land. The land of the tribe or family was held in common—it was the common property of all—and the Brehon or judge divided it, and gave to each man what was necessary for him, with free right of pasturage over the whole. They had no idea of slavery or serfdom amongst them. The Irish clansman was of the same blood with his chieftain. O'Brien that sat in the saddle at the head of his men was related to gallowglass O'Brien that was in the ranks. No such thing as looking down by the chieftains upon their people; no such thing as a cowed, abject submission upon the part of the people to a tyrannical chieftain. In the ranks they stood as freemen—perfectly equal, one with the other. We are told by Gerald Barry, the lying historian—who sometimes, though rarely, told the truth—that when the English came to Ireland nothing astonished them more than the free and bold manner in which the humblest man spoke to his chieftain, and the condescending kindness and spirit of equality with which the chieftain treated the humblest soldier in his tribe.

This was the ancient Irish Constitution, my friends. And now, does this look anything like anarchy? Can it be said with truth of a land where the laws were so well defined, where everything was in its proper place—that there was anarchy? Mr. Froude says, "There was anarchy there, because the chieftains were fighting amongst themselves." So they were; but, he also adds: "There was fighting everywhere in Europe after the breaking up of the Roman Empire." Well, Mr. Froude! fighting was going on everywhere; the Saxons were fighting the Normans around them in England; and what right have you to say that Ireland, beyond all other nations, was given up to anarchy, because chieftain drew the sword against chieftain frequently from time to time?'

So much for the question of government. Now, for the question of religion. The Catholic religion flourished in Ireland for six hundred years and more before the Anglo-Normans invaded her coasts. For the first three hundred years, that religion was the glory of the world and the pride of God's holy Church. Ireland for these three hundred years was the island mother-home of saints and of scholars. Men came from every country in the then known world to light the lamps of knowledge and of sanctity at the sacred fire upon the altars of Ireland. Then came the Danes, and for three hundred years our people were harassed by incessant war. The

Danes, as Mr. Froude remarks, apparently with a great deal of approval, had no respect for Christ or for religion, and the first thing they did was to set fire to the churches and monasteries. The nuns and holy monks were scattered, and the people left without instruction. In time of war men don't have much time to think of religion or things of peace. And for three hundred years Ireland was subject to the invasions of the Danes. On Good Friday morning, in the year 1014, Brian Boroihme defeated the Danes at Clontarf, but it was not until the 23d of August, 1103, in the twelfth century, that the Danes were driven out of the land by the defeat of Magnus, their king, at Lough Strangford, in the north of Ireland. The consequence of these Danish wars was that the Catholic religion, though it remained in all its vital strength, in all the purity of its faith amongst the Irish people, yet it remained sadly shorn of that sanctity which adorned it for the first three hundred years of Irish Christianity. Vices sprang up amongst the people, for they were accustomed to war, war, night and day, for three centuries. Where is the people on the face of the earth that would not be utterly demoralized by fifty years of war, much less by three hundred? "The Wars of the Roses" in England did not last more than thirty years, and they left the English people so demoralized that almost without a struggle they changed their religion at the dictates of the blood-thirsty and licentious tyrant, Henry VIII.* No sooner was the Dane gone than the Irish people summoned their bishops and their priests to council, and we find almost every year after the final expulsion of the Danes a council held. Here gathered the bishops, priests, the leaders and the chieftains of the land—the heads of the great septs or families. There they made those laws by which they endeavored to repair all the evils of the Danish invasion. Strict laws of Christian morality were enforced, and again and again we find these councils assembled to receive a Papal Legate—Cardinal Paparo, in the year 1164, four years before the Norman invasion. They invited the Papal Legate to their councils, and we find the Irish people every year before the Norman invasion obeying the laws of these councils without a murmur. We find councils of Irish bishops assembled, supported by the sword and power of the chieftains, with the Pope's Legate, who was received into Ireland with open arms whenever his master sent him, and without let or hindrance. When he arrived he was surrounded with all the devotion and chivalrous affection which the Irish have always paid to the representatives of their religion in the country. And, my friends, it is worth our while to see what was the consequence of all these councils—what was the result of this great religious revival which was taking place in Ireland during the few years that elapsed between the last Danish invasion and the invasion of the Normans. We find three Irish saints reigning together in the church. We find St. Malachi, one of the greatest saints, Primate of Armagh. We find him succeeded by St. Celsus, and again by Gregorius, whose name is a name high up in the martyrology of the time. We find in Dublin St. Laurence O'Toole of glorious memory. We find Felix and Christian, Bishops of Lismore; Catholicus, of Down; Augustine, of Waterford; every man of them famed not only in Ireland but throughout the whole Church of God for the greatness of their learning and for the brightness of their sanctity. We find at the same time Irish monks, famous for their learning as men of their day, and as famous for their sanctity. In the great Irish Benedictine monastery of Ratisbon, we find Dionysius, Isaac, Gervase, Conrad, Marianus, Christian, and Gregory. Maurus and twelve other Irish monks in the monastery of Maniurgghen. Macurius with twelve Irish companions at Wurzburg; all of them men celebrated for their holiness and learning. We find, moreover, that the very year before the Normans arrived in Ireland, in 1168, a great council was held at Athboy, thirteen thousand Irishmen representing the nation; thirteen thousand warriors on horseback attended the council of the bishops and priests, with their chiefs, to take the law they made from them, and hear whatever the Church commanded them to obey. What was the result of all this? Ah! my friends, I am not speaking from any prejudiced point of view. It has been said "that if Mr. Froude gives the history of Ireland from an outside view, of course Father Burke would have to give it from an inside view." Now, I am not giving it from an inside view. I am only quoting English authorities. I find, in this very interval between the Danish and Saxon invasions, Lanfranc, Archbishop of Canterbury, writing to O'Brien, King of Munster, congratulating him on the religious spirit of his people. I find St. Anselm, one of the greatest saints that ever lived, and Archbishop of Canterbury under William Rufus, writing to the King of Munster; "I give thanks to God," he says, "for the many good things we hear of your Highness, and especially for the profound peace which the subjects of your realm enjoy. All good men who hear this give thanks to God and pray that He may grant you length of days."* The man that wrote that, perhaps, was thinking while he was writing of the awful anarchy, impiety, and darkness of the most dense and terrible kind which covered his own land of England in the reign of the Red King, William Rufus. And yet we are told indeed by Mr. Froude—a good judge he seems to be of religion, for he says in one of his lectures: "Religion is a thing of which one man knows as much as another, and none of us know anything at all"—that the Irish were without religion, at the very time when the Irish Church was forming itself into the model of sanctity which it was at the time of the Danish invasion, when Roderic O'Connor, King of Connaught, was acknowledged by every prince and chieftain in the land to be the high king or Ardrigh. Now, as far as regards what he says: "That Ireland was without morality," I have but little to say. I will answer this by one fact. A King of Ireland stole another man's wife. His name, accursed! was Dermot MacMurragh, King of Leinster. Every chieftain in Ireland, every man rose up, and banished him from Irish soil as unworthy to live on it. If these were the immoral people; if these were the bestial, incestuous, depraved race which they are described by leading Norman authorities, may I ask you might not King Dermot turn round and say: "Why are you making war upon me; is it not the order of the day? Have I not as good a right to be faithless as anybody else?" Now comes Mr. Froude and says, "The Normans were sent to Ireland to teach the Ten Commandments to the Irish." In the language of Shakespeare I would say—"Oh! Jew, I thank thee for that word." In these Ten Commandments the three most important are, in their relation to human society, "Thou shalt not steal; thou shalt not kill; thou shalt not covet thy neighbor's wife." The Normans, even in Mr. Froude's view, had no right or title under Heaven to one square inch of the soil of Ireland. They came to take what was not their own, what they had no right, no title to. And they came as robbers and thieves to teach the Ten Commandments to the Irish people, amongst them the commandment "Thou shalt not steal." Henry landed in Ireland in 1171. He was after murdering the holy Archbishop of Canterbury, St. Thomas à Becket. They scattered his brains before the foot of the altar, before the Blessed Sacrament, at the vesper hour. The blood of the saint and martyr was upon his hands when he came to Ireland to teach the Irish, "Thou shalt not kill."

What was the occasion of their coming? When the adulterer was driven from the sacred soil of Erin, as one unworthy to profane it by his tread, he went over to Henry and procured from him a letter permitting any of his subjects that chose to embark for Ireland to do so, and there to reinstate the adulterous tyrant, King Dermot, in his kingdom. They came then as protectors and helpers of adultery to teach the Irish people, "Thou shalt not covet thy neighbor's wife."

Mr. Froude tells us they were right—that they were the apostles of purity, honesty, and clemency, and Mr. Froude "is an honorable man." Ah! but he says, "remember, my good Dominican friend, that if they came to Ireland, they came because the Pope sent them." Henry, in the year 1175, produced a letter which he said he received from Pope Adrian IV., which commissioned him to go to Ireland, and permitted him there, according to the terms of the letter, to do whatever he thought right and fit to promote the glory of God and the good of the people. The date that was on the letter was 1155, consequently it was twenty years old. During the twenty years nobody ever heard of that letter except Henry, who had it in his pocket, and an old man called John of Salisbury, that wrote how he went to Rome and procured the letter in a huggermugger way from the Pope. Now, I solemnly and fearlessly assert that the letter was a forgery, and that Pope Adrian never issued any such document. This letter or brief comes down to us on the authority of John of Salisbury, who tells us in a work of his called "Metalogicus," that being in Rome in 1155, he obtained from Pope Adrian the investiture of Ireland for Henry II. This statement is made in the last chapter of the book. It has no bearing on the subject matter, or context of the work, and at first sight looks like a kind of after-thought, let in apropos of nothing. The "Metalogicus" must have been written about the year 1159, for the author tells us that he had just received the news of Adrian's death, which took place in that year. Moreover, he states that Theobald, Archbishop of Canterbury, was still living, and Theobald died in 1161. If, then, the assertion in question was in the Metalogicus of John of Salisbury, it must have seen the light in 1159 or 1160. But all historians acknowledge without a shadow of doubt that Adrian's letter was never published nor heard of until 1174 or 1175, therefore, I conclude that it is a forged document, let into a subsequent edition of the Metalogicus when John of Salisbury was dead and gone.

Moreover, the brief of Adrian, as we find in the ancient manuscripts, was dated from Rome, but Pope Adrian was not in Rome at all during that time. Immediately after his consecration he had to fly from Rome, on account of popular commotions excited and led by the celebrated Arnold of Brescia; and John of Salisbury himself attests that he found the Pope at Benevento, where he stayed with him for three months. How comes it, therefore, that Adrian's brief should date from Rome when the Pope was not there at all?

How comes it that John of Salisbury, in his book called "Polycratius," in which he deals *ex professo* with his visit to Adrian, does not mention one word about the celebrated brief?

But, replies Mr. Froude, we have another document which places the authenticity of Adrian's letter beyond all question. We have the bull of Pope Alexander III., acknowledging and confirming Adrian's grant?

This opens the question—is the bull of Alexander genuine. We have it on the authority of Gerald Barry, commonly called Giraldus Cambrensis, one of the greatest liars that ever put pen to paper, as all students of history well know. Pope Alexander wrote three letters in 1172, which are certainly authentic. One was addressed to the Irish bishops, another to the Irish chieftains, and a third to King Henry himself. These three letters treat entirely and exclusively, of the invasion of Ireland, and nowhere do we find one word about Adrian's concession of the island. The only title they recognize in Henry is, "that monarch's power and the submission of the Irish chieftains." At the time these letters were written no man in Ireland had ever heard of Adrian's grant, for, if it existed, Henry up to this time had kept it carefully concealed. These three genuine letters were dated from Tusculum and not from Rome. The bull on which Mr. Froude relies is a fourth document of the same year, 1172, and it is dated *from Rome*. Now, Pope Alexander was not in Rome in 1172, nor for six years later, and any papal document dated from Rome in that year is a forgery.

Giraldus inserted the bull of Pope Alexander in his book on the conquest of Ireland, "Expugnatio Hibernica;" but did he believe in it himself? We have another work of his written some years after, and entitled "De Principis Instructione," in which, speaking of Alexander's bull, he says, "Some assert or imagine that this bull was obtained from the Pope; but others deny that it was ever obtained from the Pontiff." Amongst the "others" were the whole Irish priesthood and people, who very properly have always looked upon these two supposed papal documents as audacious Norman forgeries. "It will be well also," observes the learned Bishop of Ossory, "whilst forming our judgment regarding this supposed bull of Adrian, to hold in mind the disturbed state of society, especially in Italy, at the time to which it refers. At the present day it would be no easy matter indeed for such a forgery to survive more than a few weeks. But at the close of the twelfth century it was far otherwise. Owing to the constant revolutions and disturbances that then prevailed, the Pontiff was oftentimes obliged to fly from city to city; frequently his papers were seized and burned, and he himself detained as a hostage or prisoner by his enemies. Hence it is that several forged bulls, examples of which are given in 'Cambrensis Eversus,' date from these times. More than one of the grants made to the Norman families are now believed to rest on such forgeries; and that the Anglo-Norman adventurers in Ireland were not strangers to such deeds of darkness appears from the fact that a matrix forging the Papal Seal of such bulls, now preserved in the R. I. Academy, was found a few years ago in the ruins of one of the earliest Anglo-Norman monasteries, founded by De Courcy."

"The circumstances of the publication of the bull by Henry were surely not calculated to disarm suspicion. Our opponents do not even pretend that it was made known in Ireland till the year 1775, and hence, though publicly granted with solemn investiture, as John of Salisbury's testimony would imply, and though its record was deposited in the public archives of the kingdom, this bull, so vital to the interests of the Irish Church, should have remained dormant for twenty years, unnoticed in Rome, unnoticed by Henry's courtiers, still more, unnoticed by the Irish bishops, and, I will add, unnoticed by the Continental sovereigns, so jealous of the power and preponderance of the English monarch. For such suppositions there is indeed no parallel in the whole history of investitures."

But Mr. Froude will doubtless say you may see the copy of Adrian's bull in Baronius's Annuals, copied "from a Vatican manuscript." I answer, the manuscript in question is merely the history of Matthew of Paris, an English monk of St. Albans. But nowhere in the private archives, or among the private papers of the Vatican, or in the authoritative "Regesta," or in the various indices of the pontifical letters, can a single trace be found of the supposed bulls of Adrian IV. and Alexander III.

"There is only one other reflection," continues the learned Bishop of Ossory, " with which I wish to detain the reader. The condition of our country, and the relations between Ireland and the English king, which are set forth in the supposed bull, are precisely those of the year 1172; but it would have required more than a prophetic vision to have anticipated them in 1155. In 1155 Ireland was not in a state of turmoil or verging towards barbarism; on the contrary, it was rapidly progressing, and renewing its claim to religious and moral pre-eminence. I will add, that Pope Adrian, who had studied under Irish masters, knew well this flourishing condition of our country. In 1172, however, a sad change had come over our island. Four years of continual warfare, and the ravages of the Anglo-Norman fillibusters, since their first landing in 1168, had well nigh reduced Ireland to a state of barbarism, and the authentic letters of Alexander III., in 1172, faithfully describe its most deplorable condition. Moreover, an expedition of Henry to Ireland, which would not be an invasion, and yet would merit the homage of the Irish princes, was simply an impossibility in 1155. But owing to the special circumstances of the kingdom, such in reality was the expedition of Henry in 1172. He set out for Ireland, not avowedly to invade and conquer it, but to curb the insolence and to punish the deeds of pillage of his own Norman freebooters. Hence, during his stay in Ireland he fought no battle and made no conquest; his first measures of severity were directed against some of the most lawless of the early Norman adventurers, and this, more than anything else, reconciled the native princes to his military display. In return he received from a majority of the Irish chieftains the empty title of *Ard-righ*, or "Head Sovereign," which did not suppose any conquest on his part, and did not involve any surrender of their own hereditary rights. Such a state of things could not have been imagined in 1155; and yet it is one which is implied in the spurious bull of the much maligned Pontiff, Adrian IV."

It is said Adrian gave the rescript, and did not know the man he gave it to. But Alexander knew him well! Henry, in 1159 and 1166, supported the anti-Popes against Alexander, and, according to Matthew of Westminster, King Henry II. obliged every one in England, from the boy of twelve years of age to the old man, to renounce their allegiance to Alexander III., and go over to the anti-Popes. Now is it likely that Alexander would give him a rescript, telling him to go to Ireland and settle the ecclesiastical matters there? Alexander himself wrote to Henry, and said to him, "Instead of remedying the disorders caused by your predecessors, you have added prevarication to prevarication; you have oppressed the Church, and endeavored to destroy the canons of apostolical men."

Such is the man that Alexander sent to Ireland to

make the Irish good people. According to Mr. Froude, the Irish never loved the Pope until the Normans taught them."[10] What is the fact? Until the accursed Norman came to Ireland, the Papal Legate always came to the land at his pleasure. No king ever obstructed him; no Irish hand was ever raised against a bishop or priest of the land, or Papal Legate. After, the Legate Cardinal Vivian came to England; Henry took him by the throat and made him swear that when he went to Ireland he would do nothing against the interest of the king. It was an unheard of thing that archbishops and cardinals should be persecuted, until the Normans taught the world how to do it, with their accursed feudal system, concentrating all power in the king.

Ah, bitterly did Laurence O'Toole feel it—the great, heroic saint of Ireland—when he went to England on his last voyage! The moment he arrived in England, the king's officers made him prisoner. The king had left orders that he was never to set foot in Ireland again.

It was this man that was sent over as an apostle of morality to Ireland; he was the man accused of violating the betrothed wife of his own son, Richard I.; a man whose crimes will not bear repetition; a man who was believed by Europe to be possessed of the devil; a man of whom it is written "that when he got into a fit of anger, he tore off his clothes and sat naked, chewing straw like a beast!" Furthermore, is it likely that a Pope who knew him so well, who suffered so much from him, would have sent him to Ireland—the murderer of bishops, the robber of churches, the destroyer of ecclesiastical liberty, and of every form of liberty that came before him? No! I never will believe that the Pope of Rome was so very short-sighted, so unjust, as, by a stroke of his pen, to abolish and destroy the liberties of the most faithful people who ever bowed down in allegiance to him."

But let us suppose that Pope Adrian gave the bull. I hold still it was of no account, because it was obtained under false pretences; for he told the Pope that the Irish people were in a state of miserable ignorance, which did not exist. Thus, he told a lie, and, according to the Roman law, a papal rescript obtained on a lie is null and void. Again, when Henry told the Pope when he gave him that rescript and power to go to Ireland, that he would fix everything right, and do everything for the glory of God and the good of the people, he had no intention of doing it and never did it. Consequently, the rescript was null and void.

But suppose the rescript was valid. Well, my friends, what power did it give Henry? Did it give him the land of Ireland? Not a bit of it. Any one who attentively weighs the words of the document will see at once that it prescinds from all title of conquest, whilst at the same time it makes no gift or transfer of dominion to Henry II. As far as this letter of Adrian is concerned, the visit of Henry to our island might be the enterprise of a friendly monarch, who, at the invitation of a distracted state, would seek by his presence to restore peace, and to uphold the observance of the laws. Thus, those foolish theories must at once be set aside, which rest on the groundless supposition that Pope Adrian authorized the invasion and plunder of our people by the Anglo-Norman adventurers. At most, all he said he wished of the Irish chieftains was to acknowledge Henry's high sovereignty over the land. Now, you must know that in these early middle ages there were two kinds of sovereignty. There was a sovereignty that had the people and the land. They were the king's; he governed these as the kings and emperors do in Europe to-day. Besides this real sovereignty there was what was called a "*haute suzeraineté*" or high dominion, which required the homage only of the chieftains of the land, but which left them in perfect liberty, and in perfect independence. Henry demanded this nominal tribute of their homage, and nothing more. This was all evidently that the Pope of Rome intended in Ireland, if he permitted so much; and the proof of it lies here, that when Henry II. came to Ireland he did not claim of the Irish kings that they should give up their sovereignty. He left Roderic O'Connor King of Connaught, acknowledging him as a fellow-king; he acknowledged his royalty, and confirmed him when he demanded of him the allegiance and the homage of a feudal prince—a feudal suzerain —leaving him in perfect independence.

Again, let us suppose that Henry intended to conquer Ireland, and bring it into slavery. Did he succeed?

Was there a conquest at all? Nothing like it. He came to Ireland; the kings and princes of the Irish people said to him: "Well, we are willing to acknowledge your high sovereignty. You are the lord of Ireland, but we are the owners of the land. It is simply acknowledging your title as lord of Ireland, and nothing more." If he intended anything more, he never carried out his intention; he was able to conquer that portion which was held before by the Danes, but nothing more. It is a fact that when the Irish had driven the Danes out of Ireland at Clontarf, that, as they always were straightforward and generous in the hour of their triumph, they permitted the Danes to remain in Dublin, Wexford, Wicklow, and Waterford. The consequence of this was that a good portion of the eastern seaboard of Ireland was in the possession of the Danes. The Normans came over, and were regarded by the Irish as cousins to the Danes, and only took the Danish territory—nothing more—and the Irish seemed willing to share with them. Mr. Froude's second justification of these most iniquitous acts is, that Ireland was a prey to the Danes. He says the Danes came to the land and made the people ferocious, and leaves his hearers to infer that the Danish wars in Ireland were only a succession of individual and ferocious contests between tribe and tribe, and between man and man, whereas they were a magnificent trial of strength between two of the greatest and bravest nations that ever met foot to foot or hand to hand on a battlefield. The Danes were unconquerable in every other land which they invaded; the Celts, for three hundred years, fought with them and disputed every inch of the land with them, filled every valley in the land with their dead bodies, and in the end drove them back into the North Sea, and freed their native soil from their domination. This magnificent contest is represented by this historian as a mere ferocious onslaught, daily renewed betwen man and man in Ireland. The Normans arrived and we have seen how they were received; the Butlers and Fitzgeralds went down into Kildare; the De Berminghams and Burkes went down into Connaught. The people offered them very little opposition, gave them a portion of their lands, and welcomed them amongst them; and they began to love them as if they were their own flesh and blood. That love was soon returned. But, my friends, these Normans, so haughty in England, despised the Saxons so bitterly that their name for the Saxon was "villein" or churl. They would not allow a Saxon to sit at the same table with them, and never thought of intermarrying with the Saxons for many long years. The proud Norman, ferocious in his passions, brave as a lion, formed by his Crusades and Saracenic wars, the bravest warrior of his times—this steel-clad knight disdained the Saxon. Even one of their followers, Gerald Barry, speaking of the Saxons, says: "I am a Welshman; who would think of comparing the Welsh with the Saxon boors, the basest race on the face of the earth?" (I am only giving his words—not sharing in his sentiments.) They fought one battle, and when the Normans conquered them they consented to be slaves forevermore. Who would compare them with the Welsh—the Celtic race? says this man: with the brave, intellectual, and magnanimous race of the Celts. Now, my friends, when these Normans went down into Ireland amongst the Irish people, went out from the Danish portion of the Pale, what is the first thing that we see? They threw off their Norman traits, forgot their Norman-French language and took the Irish, took Irish wives—and were glad to get them—and adopted Irish customs, until in two hundred years after the Norman invasion, we find these proud descendants of William Fitzaldem, Earl of Clanricarde, changing their names, for my name of Burke was changed to the upper and lower McWilliam, or sons of William, in the days of Lionel, Duke of Clarence, and so they called themselves by the name and adopted the language and customs of the country. Of the four hundred sad years that followed the Norman invasion down to the accession of Henry VIII., Mr. Froude has nothing to say, except that Ireland was in a constant state of anarchy and confusion; and it is too true. It is perfectly true. Chieftain against chieftain. It was comparative peace before the invasion, but when the Normans came in they divided them by craft and cunning. The ancient historian, Strabo, says: "The Gauls always march openly to their end, and they are therefore easily circumvented." So when the Normans came, and the Saxons, they sowed dissensions among the people. They stirred them up against each other, and the bold, hot blood of the Celt was always ready to engage in contest and in war. What was the secret of that incessant and desolating war? There is no history more painful to read than the history of the Irish people, from the day that the Norman landed on their coast until the day when the great issue of Protestantism was put before the nation, and when Irishmen rallied in that grand day as one man. My friends, the true secret of the early and constant efforts of the English to force upon Ireland the establishment of the feudal system, was to rob the Irish of every inch of their land and to exterminate the Celtic race."[2] I lay this down as the one secret, the one thread by which you may unravel the tangled skein of our history for the four hundred years that followed the Norman invasion. The Normans and the Saxons came with the express purpose and design of taking every foot of land in Ireland, and exterminating the Celtic race. It is an awful thing to think of, but we have evidence for it. First of all, Henry II., whilst he made his treaties with the Irish kings, secretly divided the whole of Ireland into ten portions, and allotted each of these portions to one of his Norman knights. In a word, he robbed the Irish people, and the Irish chieftains, of every foot of land in the Irish territory. It is true, the invaders were not able to take possession. It is as if a master robber were to divide the booty before it is taken. It is far easier to assign property not yet stolen, than to put the thieves into possession of it. There were Irish hands and Irish battle-blades in the way for many a long year, nor has it been accomplished to this day. In order to root out the Celtic race, and to destroy us, mark the measures of legislation which followed. First of all, my friends, whenever an Englishman was put in possession of an acre of land, he got the right to trespass upon his Irish neighbors, and to take their land, as far as he could, and they had no action in a court of law to recover their land. If an Irishman brought an action at law against an Englishman, for taking half of his field, or for trespassing upon his land, according to the law from the very beginning, that Irishman was sent out of court—there was no action—the Englishman was perfectly justified. Worse than this. They made laws declaring that the killing of an Irishman was no felony. Sir John Davis tells us how, upon a certain occasion, at the assizes at Waterford, in the twenty-ninth year of Edward I., a certain Thomas Butler brought an action against Robert de Almain, to recover certain goods that Robert had stolen from him. The cause was brought into court. Robert acknowledged that he had stolen the goods; that he was a thief. The defense he put in was that Edward, the man he had plundered, was an Irishman. Now, my friends, just think of it! The issue that was put before the jury was not whether the robbery was really committed, but whether Edward, the plaintiff, was an Irishman, or an Englishman. Robert, the thief, was obliged to give back the goods—for the jury found that Edward was an Englishman. But if the jury found that Edward was an Irishman, he might go without the goods—there was no action against the thief, if the man aggrieved happened not to be of the thief's nation. We find upon the same authority—Sir John Davis—a description of a certain jail delivery at Waterford, where a man named Robert Welsh killed an Irishman, John, the son of Ivor McGilmore. He was arraigned and tried for manslaughter, and he, without the slightest difficulty, acknowledged it. "Yes, I did kill him," said he; "you cannot try me for it, however, as he was only an Irishman!" Instantly he was let out of the dock, on condition—as the Irishman was in the service at the time of an English master—he should pay whatever he compelled him to pay for the loss of his services, and the murderer might go scot-free."[18] Not only, says Sir John Davis, were the Irish considered aliens, but they were considered enemies, insomuch that though an Englishman might settle upon an Irishman's land, there was no redress; but if an Irishman wished to buy an acre of land from an Englishman he could not do it. So they kept the land they had and they were always adding to it by plunder: they could steal without even buying more. On the other hand, the Irish were forbid even to purchase land. Though the English might take from the Irish, the Irish could not, even by way of gift or purchase, take any from the English. In every charter of English liberty, as it was called, granted to an Irishman, besides the right to bring actions in the king's court, there was given an express power to him to purchase lands for himself and heirs. Without this he could not hold any so acquired. If any man made a will, and left an acre of land to an Irishman, the moment it was proved that he was an Irishman, the land was forfeited to the Crown of England—even if it was only left in trust to him, as we have two very striking examples. We read that a certain James Butler left some lands in Meath in trust for charitable purposes, and he left them to his two chaplains. It was proved that the two priests were Irishmen, and that it was left to them in trust for charitable purposes; yet the land was forfeited because the trustees were Irishmen. Later, a certain Mrs. Catharine Dowdall, a pious woman, made a will, leaving some land, also for charitable purposes, to her chaplain, and the land was forfeited because the priest was an Irishman.

In the year 1367, Lionel, Duke of Clarence, a third son of Edward III., came to Ireland, held a parliament in Kilkenny, and passed certain laws. You will scarcely believe what I am going to tell you. Some of these were as follows: If any man speaks the Irish language, or keeps company with the Irish, or adopts Irish customs, his lands shall be taken from him and forfeited to the Crown of England. If an Englishman married an Irish woman, what do you think was the penalty? He was sentenced to be half hanged; to have his heart cut out before he was dead, and to have his head struck off, and every right to his land passed to the Crown of England. Thus, says

Sir John Davis, it is evident that the constant design of English legislation in Ireland was to possess the Irish lands, and to extirpate and exterminate the Irish people.

Now, citizens of America, Mr. Froude came here to appeal to you for your verdict, and he asks you to say: Was not England justified in her treatment of Ireland because the Irish people would not submit? Now, citizens of America, would not the Irish people be the vilest dross on the face of the earth if they submitted to such treatment as this? Would they be worthy of the name of men if they submitted to be robbed, plundered, and degraded? It is true that, in all this legislation, we see this same spirit of contempt of which I spoke in the beginning of my lecture. But remember it was not Saxon churls that were thus despised, and ask yourselves what race they treated with so much contumely and attempted in every way to degrade whilst they were ruining and robbing them. Spencer, speaking of the Irish race, says: "The Irish are one of the most ancient nations that I know of at this end of the world, and come of as mighty a race as the world ever brought forth." He knew of no people more valiant and more intellectual. Those who came over from England were called, by their own countrymen in Ireland, Saxon hobs, or churls, while the Irish called them *Buddagh Sassenach*. These were the men who showed, in the very system by which they were governed, that they could not understand the genius of freedom; that they could not understand the nature of a people who refused to be slaves. They were slaves themselves. Consider the nature of the feudal system under which they lived. According to the feudal system of government, the King of England was lord of every inch of land in England. Every foot of land in England was the king's, and the nobles who had the land held it from the king—held it under feudal conditions, the most degrading that can be imagined. For instance, if a man died and left his heir, a son or daughter, under age, the heir or heiress, together with the estate, went into the hands of the king. He might perhaps leave a widow with ten children. She would have to support all the children herself out of her dower, but the estate and the eldest son or the eldest daughter went into the hands of the king. Then, during their minority, the king could spend the revenues or could sell the castle and sell the estate without being questioned by any one; and when the son or daughter came of age, he then sold them in marriage to the highest bidder. We have Godfrey of Mandeville buying for twenty thousand marks, from King John, the hand of Isabella, Countess of Gloster. We have Isabella de Linjera, another heiress, offering two hundred marks to King John—for what?—for liberty to marry whoever she liked, and not be obliged to marry the man he would give her. If a widow lost her husband, the moment the breath was out of him the lady and the estate were in the king's or suzerain's possession, and he might squander the estate or do whatever he liked with it, and then he could sell the woman. We have a curious example of this. We find Alice, Countess of Warwick, paying King John one thousand pounds sterling in gold for leave to remain a widow as long as she liked, and then to marry any one she liked. This was the slavery called the feudal system, of which Mr. Froude is so proud, and of which he says: It lay at the root of most that is noble and good in Europe. The Irish could not understand it—small blame to them. But when the Irish people found that they were to be hunted down like wolves—found their lands were to be taken from them and that there was no redress, over and over again the Irish people sent up petitions to the King of England to give them the benefit of the English law, and they would be amenable to it; but they were denied and told that they should remain as they were, that is to say, England was determined to extirpate them, and get every foot of Irish soil. This is the one leading idea or principle which animated England in her treatment of Ireland throughout those four hundred years, and it is the only clue you can find to that turmoil, and misery, and constant fighting which was going on in Ireland during that time. Sir James Cusack, the English Commissioner sent over by Henry VIII., wrote to his Majesty these quaint words: "The Irish be of opinion amongst themselves that the English wish to get all their lands, and to root them out completely." He just struck the nail on the head. Mr. Froude himself acknowledges that the land question lies at the root of the whole business. Nay, more, the feudal system would have handed over every inch of land in Ireland to the Norman king and his Norman nobles, and the O'Briens, the O'Tooles, the O'Donnells and the O'Connors were of more ancient and better blood than that of William, the bastard Norman.

The Saxon might submit to feudal law and be crushed into a slave, a clod of the earth—the Celt never could. England's great mistake—in my soul I am convinced that the great mistake, of all others the greatest—lay in this, that the English people never realized the fact that in dealing with the Irish they had to deal with the proudest race upon the face of the earth. During these wars the Norman earls, the Ormonds, the Desmonds, the Geraldines, the De Burghes, were at the head and front of every rebellion. The English complained of them, and said they were worse than the Irish rebels; that they were constantly stirring up disorders. Do you know the reason why? Because they, as Normans, were under the feudal laws, and therefore the king's sheriff would come down on them at every turn with fines and forfeitures of the land held from the king. So, by keeping the country in disorder, they were always able to elude the sheriffs, and they preferred the Irish freedom to the English feudalism—therefore, they fomented and kept up these discords. It was the boast of my kinsmen of Clanricarde that, with the blessing of God, they would never allow a king's writ to run in Connaught. Dealing with this period of our history, Mr. Froude says that the Irish chieftains and their septs or tribes were doing this or that mischief, the Geraldines, the Desmonds, and the Ormonds. I say in reply to this, that the Geraldines and the Ormonds were not the Irish people, so don't father their acts upon the Irish; the Irish chieftains have enough to answer for. During these four hundred years, I protest to you that in this most melancholy period of our sad history I have found but two cases, two instances, that cheer me; and both were the action of native Irish chieftains. In one we find that in 1339, Turlough O'Connor put away his lawful wife Dervail, daughter of Hugh O'Donnell of Tyrconnel, and took to him the daughter of Turlough O'Brien. With the spirit of their heroic ancestors, the Irish chieftains of Connaught came together, deposed him, and drove him out of the place in 1342, after three years' incessant warfare. Later on we find another chieftain, Brian McMahon, who induced Sorley McDonnell, chief of the Hebrides, to put away his lawful wife and marry a daughter of his own. The following year they fell out, and McMahon drowned his own son-in-law. The chiefs, O'Donnell and O'Neill, came together with their forces and deposed McMahon, in the cause of virtue, honor, and womanhood. I have looked in vain through these four hundred years for one single trait of generosity or of the assertion of virtue among the Anglo-Norman chiefs, and the dark picture is only relieved by these two gleams of Irish patriotism and Irish zeal in the cause of virtue, honor, and purity.

Now, my friends, Mr. Froude opened another question in his first lecture. All this time, while the English monarchs were engaged in trying to subjugate Scotland and subdue their French provinces, the Irish were rapidly gaining ground, coming in and entering the Pale year by year; the English power in Ireland was in danger of annihilation, and the only thing that saved it was the love of the Irish for their own independent way of fighting, which, though favorable to freedom, was hostile to national unity. He says, speaking of that time, Would it not have been better to have allowed the Irish chieftains to govern their own people, and give the Irish their freedom? And he answers, Freedom to whom?—freedom to the bad, to the violent? It is no freedom. I deny that the Irish chieftains, with all their faults, were, as a class, bad men or violent men. I deny that they were engaged, as Mr. Froude says, in cutting their people's throats, that they were a people who would never be satisfied. Mr. Froude tells us emphatically and significantly, that "the Irish people were satisfied with their chieftains," but people are not satisfied under a system where their throats are being cut. The Irish chieftains were the bane of Ireland by their divisions; the Irish chieftains were the ruin of their country by their want of union and want of generous acquiescence to some great and noble head that would save them by uniting them. The Irish chieftains, even in the days of the heroic Edward Bruce, did not rally around him as they ought. In their divisions is the secret of Ireland's slavery and ruin through those years. But with all that, history attests that they were still magnanimous enough to be the fathers of their people, and to be the natural leaders, as God intended them to be, of their septs, families, and namesakes. And they struck whatever blow they did strike in what they imagined to be the cause of right, justice, and principle, and the only blow that came in the cause of outraged honor and purity, came from the hands of the Irish chiefs, in those dark and dreadful years.

Now, I will endeavor to follow this learned gentleman in his subsequent lectures. Now a darker cloud than that of mere invasion is lowering over Ireland; now comes the demon of religious discord—the sword of religious persecution waving over the distracted and exhausted land. And we shall see whether this historian has entered into the spirit of the great contest that followed, and that in our day has ended in a glorious victory for Ireland's Church and Ireland's nationality, and which will be followed as assuredly by triumphs still more glorious in the future.

# LECTURE II.

# IRELAND UNDER THE TUDORS.

LADIES AND GENTLEMEN: We now come to consider the second lecture of the eminent English historian who has come among us. It covers one of the most interesting and terrible passages in our history. It takes in three reigns—the reign of Henry VIII., the reign of Elizabeth, and the reign of James I. I scarcely consider the reign of Edward VI., or of Philip and Mary, worth counting. The learned gentleman began his second lecture with rather a startling paradox. He asserted that Henry VIII. was a hater of disorder. Now, my dear friends, every man in this world has his hero; whether consciously or unconsciously, every man selects some character out of history that he admires, until, at length, by continually dwelling on the virtues and excellencies of his hero, he comes to almost worship him. Before us all lie the grand historic names that are written in the world's annals, and every man is free to select the character that he likes best, and he thus choses his hero. Using this privilege, Mr. Froude has made the most singular selection of a hero that you or I ever heard of. His hero is Henry VIII. It speaks volumes for the integrity of Mr. Froude's own mind. It is a strong argument that he possesses a charity most sublime, when he has been enabled to discover virtues in the historical character of one of the greatest monsters that ever cursed the earth. He has, however, succeeded in this, to us, apparent impossibility; he has discovered among many other shining virtues in the character of the English Nero a great love for order, a great hatred of disorder. Well, we must stop at the very first sentence of the learned gentleman and try to analyze it and see how much there is of truth in this word of the historian, and how much there is which is honorable to him and a charitable though strange figment of his imagination. All order in the state is based upon three great principles, my friends. First, the supremacy of the law; second, respect for the existence as well as liberty of conscience; and third, a tender regard for that which lies at the fountain-head of all human society, namely, the sanctity of the marriage tie.

The first element of order in every state is the supremacy of the law, for in this supremacy lies the very quintessence of human freedom and of all order. The law is supposed to be, according to the definition of Aquinas, "the judgment pronounced by profound reason and intellect, thinking and legislating for the public good." The law, therefore, is the expression of reason—reason backed by authority, reason influenced by the noble motive of the public good. This being the nature of law, the very first thing that is demanded for the law is that every man shall bow down to it and obey it. No man in any community has any right to claim exemption from obedience to the law; least of all the man who is at the head of the community, because he is supposed to represent before the nation that principle of obedience without which all national order and happiness perishes among the people. Was Henry VIII. an upholder of the law? Was he obedient to the laws? I deny it, and I have the evidence of all history to back me up in that denial, and I brand Henry VIII. as one of the greatest enemies of freedom and law that ever lived in this world, and consequently one of the greatest tyrants. My friends, I shall only give you one example out of ten thousand which might be taken from the history of the time. When Henry VIII. broke with the Pope, he called upon his subjects to acknowledge him—bless the mark!—as spiritual head of the Church. There were three abbots of three Charter-houses in and near London, who refused to acknowledge Henry as the supreme spiritual head of the Church. He had them arrested and held for trial, and he had a jury of twelve citizens of London to sit upon them." Now, the first principle of English law, the grand palladium of English legislation and freedom, is the perfect liberty of the jury. The jury in any country must be perfectly free, not only from every form of coercion over them, but from even their own prejudice. They must be free from any prejudgment of the case; they must be perfectly impartial, and perfectly free to record the verdict at which their impartial judgment has arrived. Those twelve men refused to convict the three abbots of high treason, and they grounded their refusal upon this: Never, they said, has it been uttered in England that it was high treason to deny the spiritual supremacy of the king. It is not law, and therefore we cannot find these men guilty of high treason. What did Henry do? He sent word to the jury that if they did not find the three abbots guilty he would visit them with the same penalties which he had intended for the prisoners. He sent word to the jury that they should find them guilty. I brand Henry, therefore, with having torn in pieces the Constitution of England, Magna Charta, and of having trampled upon the first great element of law and jurisprudence, namely, the liberty of the jury. Citizens of America, would any of you like to be tried for treason by a jury of twelve men to whom the President of the United States had said that if they failed to find you guilty he would put them to death? Where would there be liberty, where would be law if such a transaction were permitted? But this was done by Mr. Froude's great admirer of order, and hero, Henry VIII.

The second grand element of order is respect for conscience. The conscience of a man, and consequently of a nation, is supposed to be the great guide in all the relations that individuals or the people bear to God. The conscience is so free that Almighty God himself respects it; and it is a theological axiom that if a man does a wrong act, thinking that he is doing right, having in his conscience invincibly the idea that he is doing right, the wrong will not be attributed to him by Almighty God. Was this man Henry a respecter of conscience? Again, out of ten thousand instances of his contempt for liberty of conscience, let me select one. He ordered the people of England to change their religion. He ordered them to give up that grand system of dogmatic teaching which is in the Catholic Church, where every man knows what to believe, and what to do. And what religion did he offer them instead? He did not offer them Protestantism, for Henry VIII. never was a Protestant, and to the last day of his life, if he had only been able to lay his hands upon Martin Luther he would have made a toast of him. He heard Mass up to the day of his death, and after his death there was a solemn High Mass over his inflated corpse—a solemn High Mass that the Lord might have mercy on his soul. Ah, my friends, some other poor soul, I suppose, got the benefit of it. What religion did he offer the people of England. He simply came before them and said: Let every man in the land agree with me; whatever I say, that is religion." More than this, his parliament—a slavish parliament, every man of which was afraid of his life—passed a law making it high treason, not only to disagree with the king in anything that he believed, but making it high treason for any man to dispute anything that the king should ever believe in a future time. He was not only the enemy of conscience; he was the annihilator of conscience. He would allow no man to have a conscience. I am your conscience, he said to the nation; I am your infallible guide in all things you are to believe and in all things you are to do; and if any man sets up his own conscience against me, he is guilty of high treason, and I will shed his heart's blood. This is the lover of order whom Mr. Froude admires. The third great element of order is that upon which all society is based. The great key-stone of society is the sanctity of the marriage tie. Whatever else you interfere with this must not be touched, for Christ our Lord himself said: "Those whom God has joined together let no man put asunder." A valid marriage can only be dissolved by the angel of death. No power in Heaven or on earth, much less in hell, can dissolve the validity of a marriage. Henry VIII. had so little respect for the sanctity of the marriage tie, that he put away from him brutally a woman to whom he was lawfully married, and took in her stead, while she was yet living, a woman who was supposed to be his own daughter. He married six wives. Two of them he repudiated—divorced; two of them he beheaded; one of them died in childbirth, and the sixth and last wife, Catherine Parr, had her name down in Henry's book, at the time of his death, amongst the list of his victims; he had made the list out, and if the monster had lived a few days longer she would have been sacrificed. This is all matter of history.

And now, I ask the American public, is it fair for Mr. Froude, or any other living man, to come and present himself before an American audience—an audience of intelligent and cultivated people, a people that have read history as well as the English historian, and ask them to believe the absurd paradox, that Henry VIII. was an admirer of order and a hater of disorder? But Mr. Froude says: Now, this is not fair. I said in my lecture that I would have nothing whatever to do with Henry's matrimonial transactions. Ah! Mr. Froude, you were wise. But at least, he says, in his relations to Ireland, I claim that he was a hater of disorder; and the proof he gives is the following. First of all, he says, that one great curse of Ireland was the absentee landlords, and he is right. Now, Henry VIII. put an end to that business in the simplest way imaginable; he took the estates from the absentees, and gave them to other people. My friends, it sounds well, very plausible, this saying of the English historian. Let us analyze it a little. During the Wars of the Roses, between the Houses of York and Lancaster, which preceded the Reformation in England, many English and Anglo-Norman families went over from Ireland to England, and joined in the conflict. It was an English question, and an English war, and the consequence was that numbers of the English settlers retired from Ireland, and left their estates—abandoned them entirely.

Others, again, from disgust, or because they had large English properties, preferred to live in their own country, and retired from Ireland to live in England. So that when Henry VIII. came to the throne of England, there remained within the boundaries of the Pale one half of Louth, West Meath, Dublin, Wicklow, and Wexford. Nothing more. Henry, according to Mr. Froude, performed a great act of justice. He took from these absentees their estates, and gave them —to whom? To other Englishmen—his own favorites and friends. Now, the historic fact is this: that the Irish people, as soon as the English retired and abandoned their estates, came in and re-possessed themselves of their own property. Mark, my friends, that even if the Irish people had no title to that property, the very fact of the English having abandoned it, gave them a sufficient title—*bona derelicta sunt primi capientis*—things that are abandoned belong to the man that gets first hold of them. But much more just was the title of the Irish people to that land, because it was their own; because they were unjustly dispossessed of it by the very men who abandoned it now; and therefore, they came in with a twofold title, namely: the land is ours because there is nobody to claim it, and even if there were, the land is ours because it was always ours, and we never lost our right to it.

When, therefore, Henry VIII., the lover of order, dispossessed the absentees of their estates, he sent over other Englishmen who would reside there, and handed over these estates to them; and remember, the enforcement of their claims involved driving the Irish people a second time out of their property. There is the whole secret of Henry VIII.'s wonderful beneficence to Ireland in giving us resident landlords. Just look at it yourselves; if you owned property—there are, doubtless, a great many here owners of property—just picture to yourselves the United States Government, or the President of the United States turning you out of your property, taking your houses and lots and land from you, and giving them to some friend of his own, and then saying to you, "Now, my friends, you must remember I am a lover of order; I have given you a resident landlord." Henry, as soon as he ascended the throne, sent over the Earl of Surrey to Ireland, in the year 1520. Surrey was a brave soldier, a stern, energetic man, and Henry thought that by sending him over to Ireland and backing him with a large army, he would be able to reduce to order the disorderly elements of the Irish nation. That disorder reigned in Ireland I am the first to admit, but in tracing this to its cause I claim that the cause was not in any inherent love for disorder in the Irish character—they were always ready to fight, I grant. But, I hold and claim that the great cause of all the disorder and turmoil of Ireland was the strange and incongruous legislation of England for four hundred years previous; and, secondly, the presence of the Anglo-Norman lords in Ireland, who were anxious to keep up the disorders in the country, in order that they might have an excuse for not paying their duties to the feudal king." Sir John Davies attorney-general of King James I. says, that "the truth is that in time of peace the Irish are more fearful to offend the law than the English or any other nation whatsoever. There is no nation of people under the sun that doth love equal and indifferent justice better than the Irish, or will rest better satisfied with the execution thereof, although it be against themselves, so that they have the protection and benefits of the law, when, upon just cause, they do desire it." Surrey came over and tried the strong hand for a time; but he found—brave as he was, and accomplished in generalship—that the Irish were a little too many for him, and he sent word to Henry: "These people," he says, "can only be subdued by conquering them utterly"— cutting off all of them by fire and sword. "Now," he says, "this you will not be able to do, because the country is too large, and because the country is so geographically fixed that it is impossible for an army to penetrate its fastnesses, and to subjugate the whole people." Then it was that Henry VIII. took up the policy of conciliation. He could not help it. Mr. Froude makes it a great virtue in Henry that he tried in this to conciliate the Irish people. He took up that policy because he had to do it, because he could not help it. Now, my friends, there is one passage in the correspondence between Surrey and Henry VIII. that speaks volumes, and it is this: When the Earl of Surrey arrived in Ireland, he found himself in the midst of war and confusion, but the people that were really the source of all that confusion, he declares, were not so much the Irish or their chiefs as the Anglo-Norman or English lords in Ireland. Here is the passage in question. There were two chieftains of the McCarthies, Cormac Oge McCarthy, and McCarthy Ruagh or Red McCarthy. Surrey writes of these two men to Henry VIII., and he says: "They are two wise men, and more conformable to order than most Englishmen were." Out of the lips of one of Ireland's bitterest enemies I take an answer to Mr. Froude's repeated allegation that the Irish are so disorderly and such lovers of turmoil and confusion, that the only way to reduce us to order is to sweep us away altogether. The next feature in Surrey's policy, when he found that he could not conquer with the sword, was to set chieftain against chieftain. And so he writes to Henry: I am endeavoring, he says, to perpetuate the animosity between O'Donnell and O'Neill of Ulster —here are his words—"for it would be dangerful to have them both agree and join together." It would be dangerous to England. Well may Mr. Froude say that in the day when we Irishmen are united, we shall be invincible, and no power on earth shall keep us slaves. "It would be dangerful to have them agree and join together, and the longer they continue in war the better it shall be for your grace's poor subjects here." Now mark the spirit of that letter. It tells the whole genius and spirit of England's treatment of Ireland. He does not speak of the Irish as the subjects of the King of England. He has not the slightest consideration for the unfortunate Irish whom they were pitting against each other. Let them bleed, he says; the longer they continue at war, and the greater number of them that are swept away, the better it will be for your grace's poor subjects here. Party legislation, party laws, intended only to protect the English settlers, and exterminate the Irishmen. This, Sir John Davis himself declared, lay at the bottom of the English legislation for Ireland for four hundred years, and was the cause of all the evils and miseries of the country. Surrey retired after two years, and then, according to Mr. Froude, Henry tried "home rule" in Ireland. Here, again, the learned historian tries to make a point for his hero. Irishmen, he says, admire the memory of this man. He tried home rule with you, and he found that you were not able to govern yourselves, and then he was obliged to take the whip and use it. Let us see what kind of home rule Henry tried. One would imagine that home rule in Ireland meant that Irishmen should manage their own affairs, make their own laws. It either means this or it means nothing. It is a delusion, a mockery, and a snare unless it means that the Irish people have a right to assemble in their parliament and govern themselves, by legislating for themselves, and making their own laws. Did Henry VIII.'s "home rule" mean this? Not a bit of it. All he did was to make the Earl of Kildare Lord Lieutenant, or Lord Deputy of Ireland, to please the Irishmen, that is to say, the Anglo-Norman Irishmen. In this consists the whole scheme of home rule attributed by Mr. Froude to Henry VIII. He did not call upon the Irish nation and say to them: Return your members to parliament, and I will allow you to make your own laws. He did not call upon the Irish chieftains—the natural representatives of the nation, the men in whose veins flowed the blood of Ireland's chieftainship for thousands of years. He did not call upon the O'Briens, the O'Neills, the McCarthymore, and the O'Connors, and say to them: Come, assemble, and make laws for yourselves, and if they are just laws, I will set my seal upon them and allow you to govern Ireland through your own legislation. No; but he set a clique of Anglo-Norman lords, the most unruly, the most lawless, and the most restless pack ever heard of or read of in all history, he set these men to take the government of the country for a time into their hands, and what was the consequence? No sooner did he leave them to govern than they began to make war on the Irish—to tear them to pieces. The first thing that Kildare does after his appointment in 1522, is to summon an army and lay waste the territories of the Irish chieftains around him, to kill their people, to burn their villages. After a time they fell out among themselves. The great Anglo-Norman family of the Butlers became jealous of Kildare, who was a Fitzgerald, and they began to accuse him of treason; and on two occasions it is really true that Kildare did carry on a treasonable correspondence, in the year 1514, with Francis I., King of France, and Charles V., Emperor of Germany. He was called to England for the third time to answer for his conduct in 1534, and there Henry put him in prison. While he was in the Tower in London, his son, Thomas Fitzgerald, who was called "Silken Thomas," a brave young man, revolted because his father was in prison, and they told him Henry intended to put him to death. Henry declared war against him, and he against the King of England, and the consequence of that war was that a portion of the province of Munster, and a great part of Leinster, was ravaged by the king's armies, the people destroyed, and the towns and villages burned, until, at length, there was not as much left as would feed man or beast. And so, under the home rule of Henry, the troubles with the Norman lords and the treason of Kildare ended in the ruin of large numbers of the Irish people. Perhaps you will ask me—Did the Irish people take part in that war so as to justify Henry's share in the awful treatment they received? I answer, they took no part in it; it was an English business from beginning to end. O'Carroll, O'More of Ossory, and O'Conor, these were the only chieftains that sided with the Geraldines at all, and drew the sword against England; and they were three chiefs of rather small importance, and by no means represented the Irish, as it was called, of Munster, or any other Irish province. And yet upon the Irish people fell the avenging hand of Henry the Eighth's armies. Mr. Froude goes on to say that "the Irish people, somehow or other, got to like Henry VIII." Well, if they did, I don't admire their taste. He pleased them, said Mr. Froude—and he assigns the reason. It was that Henry never showed any disposition to dispossess the Irish people of their lands and to exterminate them. Honest Henry! Now, I take him up on that point. Fortunately for the Irish historian, the State papers are open to us as well as to Mr. Froude. What do the State papers of the reign of Henry VIII. tell us? They tell us that project after project was formed during the reign of this monarch to drive all the Irish nation into Connaught, over the Shannon;—that Henry wished to do away with the Irish race altogether. Henry wished it, and the people of England desired it; and one of these State papers ends in these words: "Consequently the premise brought to pass, there shall no Irish be on this side of the waters of Shannon, unpersecuted, unsubjected, and unexiled; then shall the English Pale be well two hundred Irish miles long, and more." More than this, we have the evidence of the State papers of the time that Henry VIII. contemplated the utter extirpation and sweeping destruction of the whole Irish race. We find even the Lord Deputy and Council in Dublin writing to his Majesty, and suggesting to him the difficulty of realizing his design. Here are the very words: "The land is very large, by estimation as large as England, so that to inhabit the whole with new inhabitors, the number would be so great that there is no prince christened that commodiously might spare so many subjects to depart out of his regions; **but to** enterprise the **whole** extirpation **and total** destruction of **all** the Irishmen of **the land, it would be a marvellous and sumptuous** charge **and great** difficulty, considering both **the lack** of inhabitors, and the great hardness and **misery** these Irishmen can endure, both of hunger, cold and thirst, and evil lodging, more **than** the inhabitants of any other land. And by **precedent of the** conquest of this land, we have not heard **or read in any** chronicle that at such conquests **the whole inhabitants** of the lands have been utterly extirped and banished."

Great **God!** is this the man that Mr. **Froude** tells us **was the friend** of the Irish, and never showed any desire **to take** their lands and dispossess and destroy them? This is the man—the model **admirer** of order and hater of disorder. Surely he was about to create **a** magnificent order; for his idea was, **if a** people are troublesome, and you want **to** reduce them to quiet, the best way and the simplest **way is to** kill them all. Just like some of those people in England; those nurses we read **of a few** years ago, that were farming out children. When the child was a little fractious they gave him **a** nice little dose of poison, and they called it "quietness." **Do** you know the reason why Henry VIII. pleased the Irish? for there **is** no doubt about it; they were more **pleased with him** than with any English monarch up **to that time.** The reason is a very simple one. He had his own designs; but while concealing them he **was** meditating, like an anticipated **Oliver** Cromwell, **the** utter ruin and destruction of all the Irish race; but he had the good sense to keep it to himself, and he only comes out in his State papers. But he treated the Irish with a certain amount of courtesy and politeness. Henry, with all his faults, was a learned man—an accomplished man—a man of very elegant manners, a man with a bland smile, who would give you a warm shake of the hand; it is true he might the next day have your head cut off, but still he had the manners of a gentleman; and it is a singular fact, my friends, that the two most gentlemanly kings of England were the greatests coundrels that ever lived: Henry VIII. and George IV. Accordingly he dealt with the Irish people with a certain amount of civility and courtesy; he did not come amongst them like all his predecessors, saying: You are the king's enemies; you are to be all put to death; you are without the pale of the law; you are barbarians and savages; I will have nothing to say to you. Not a bit of it. Henry came and said: Let us see if we cannot arrange our difficulties, if we can't live in peace and quiet? And the Irish were charmed with the man's manners. Ah! my friends, it is true that there was a black heart under that smiling face, but it is also true, as Mr. Froude alleges, that Henry VIII. had a certain amount of popularity amongst the Irish people; which proves that if the English only knew how to treat us with respect and courtesy and with some show of kindness, they would have long since won the heart of Ireland, instead of embittering it as much by the haughtiness and stupid pride of their manner as by the injustice and cruelty of their laws. And this is what I meant when on last Tuesday evening I asserted that English contempt for Ireland is the real evil that lies deeply at the root of all the bad spirit that exists between the two nations, for the simple reason that the Irish people are too intellectual, too strong, too energetic, too pure of race and blood, too ancient and too proud to be despised.

And now, my friends, Mr. Froude went on in his lectures to give a proof of the great love that the Irish people had for Henry VIII. He says that they were so fond of this king, they actually, at the king's request, threw the Pope overboard. Now, Mr. Froude, fond as we were of your glorious hero, we were not so enamored of him, we had not fallen so deeply in love with him as to give up the Pope for him. What are the facts of the case? Henry, about the year 1530, got into difficulties with the Pope, which ended in his denying the authority and the supremacy of the head of the Catholic Church. He then picked out an apostate monk, a man who had given up his faith, a man without a shadow of either conscience, character, or virtue, and he had him consecrated the first Protestant Archbishop of Dublin. This was an Englishman by the name of Brown; and he sent George Brown over to Dublin in 1534 with a commission to get the Irish nation to follow in the wake of England, and throw the Pope overboard and acknowledge Henry's supremacy. Brown arrived in Dublin, and he called the bishops together—the bishops of the Catholic Church—and he said to them: You must change your allegiance, you must give up the Pope, and take Henry, the King of England, in his stead. The Archbishop of Armagh in these days was an Englishman; his name was Cromer; the moment he heard these words he rose up at the council board and said: What blasphemy is this I hear! Ireland will never change her faith. Ireland never will renounce her Catholicity, and she would have to do it by renouncing the head of the Catholic Church. All the bishops of Ireland followed the Primate, all the priests of Ireland followed the Primate, and George Brown wrote a most lugubrious letter home to his protector, Thomas Cromwell, telling him that he could make nothing of this people, and no doubt he would have returned to England, only he was afraid the king would have his head taken off. Three years later, however, Brown and the Lord Deputy summoned a parliament; and it was at this parliament of 1537, according to Mr. Froude, that Ireland threw the Pope overboard. Now, what are the facts? A parliament was assembled. From time immemorial in Ireland, whenever the parliament was assembled there were three delegates called proctors, from every Catholic diocese in Ireland, who sat in the House of Commons by virtue of their office. When this parliament was called, the very first thing that they did was to banish the three proctors who came from every diocese in Ireland, and to deprive them of their seats in the house. Without the slightest justice, without the slightest show or pretence of either right or law or justice, the proctors were excluded, and so the ecclesiastical element of Ireland, the Church element, was precluded from that parliament of 1537. Then, partly by bribes and partly by threats, the venal parliament of the Pale—the English Pale, the parliament of the region of the rotten little boroughs that surrounded Dublin in the five half counties—declared themselves willing to take the oath that Henry VIII. was the head of the Church; and this Mr. Froude calls the apostasy of the Irish nation. With this strange want of knowledge—for I can call it nothing else—of our religion, he attests that Ireland remained Catholic even though he asserts that she gave up the Pope. They took the oath, he says, "bishops and all took the oath of Henry VIII.'s supremacy, and they didn't become Protestants; they still remained Catholics; and the reason why they refused to take the same oath to Elizabeth, was that Elizabeth insisted upon the Protestant religion as well as the supremacy." Now I answer Mr. Froude at once to set him right on this point. The Catholic Church teaches, and has always taught, that no man is a Catholic who is not in the communion of obedience with the Pope of Rome. Henry VIII., who was a learned man, had too much logic and too much theology and too much sense to become what is called a Protestant. He never embraced the doctrines of Luther; and he held on to every iota of the Catholic doctrine to the very last day of his life, save and except that he refused to acknowledge the Pope; and on the day that Henry VIII. refused to acknowledge the Pope, Henry VIII. ceased to be a Catholic. To pretend, therefore, or to hint that the Irish people were so ignorant as to imagine that the king threw the Pope overboard and still remained a Catholic, is to offer to the genius and to the intelligence of Ireland a gratuitous insult. It is true that some five of the bishops apostatized—I can call it nothing else. They took the oath of supremacy to Henry. Their names, living in the execration of Irish history, were Eugene Maginnis, Bishop of Down and Connor; Roland Burke, I am sorry to say, Bishop of Clonfert; Florence Gerawan, Bishop of Clonmacnoise; Matthew Sanders, Bishop of Leighlin, and Hugh O'Cervallan, Bishop of Clanforth—five bishops apostatized. The rest of Ireland's episcopacy remained faithful. George Brown, the apostate Archbishop of Dublin, acknowledged his failure. Of all the priests in the diocese of Dublin, he could only persuade three to take the oath to Henry VIII. There was a priest down in Cork; he was an Irishman—a rector of Shandon—and his name was Dominick Tirrey, and he was offered the bishopric of Cork if he took the oath, and he took it. There was a man named William Miagh, another priest—he was offered the diocese of Kildare if he took the oath, and he took it. There was a man named Alexander Devereaux, abbot of Dunbrody, a Cistercian monk—he was offered the diocese of Ferns in the County Wexford, and he took it.

These are all the names that represent the national apostasy of Ireland. Eight men; out of so many hundred, eight were found wanting; and Mr. Froude turns round quietly and calmly, and tells us that the Irish bishops, priests, and people were found wanting, and threw the Pope overboard. He makes another assertion, and I regret that he made it; regret it because there is much in the learned gentleman that I admire and esteem. He asserts that the bishops of Ireland in those days were immoral men; that they had families; that they were not at all like the venerable men whom we see established in the episcopacy to-day. Now, I answer, there is not a shred of testimony to bear out Mr. Froude in this wild assertion. I have read the history of Ireland, national, civil, and ecclesiastical, as far as I could, and nowhere have I seen even an allegation, much less a proof of immorality against the Irish clergy and their bishops at the time of the Reformation. But perhaps when Mr. Froude said this of the bishops he meant the apostate bishops; if so, I am willing to grant him whatever he chooses in regard to them; and whatever charge he lays upon them, the heavier it is the more satisfied I am to see it coming.

The next passage in the relations of Henry VIII. to Ireland goes to prove that Ireland did not throw the Pope overboard. My friends, in the year 1541 a parliament assembled in Dublin and declared that Henry VIII. was King of Ireland. They had been four hundred years and more fighting for that title—

at length it was conferred by the Irish Parliament upon the English monarch. Two years later, in gratitude to the Irish Parliament, Henry called the Irish chieftains over to a grand assembly at Greenwich, and on the first of July, 1543, he gave the Irish chieftains their English titles. O'Neill of Ulster was made Earl of Tyrone; the glorious O'Donnell Earl of Tyrconnell; Ulick McWilliam Burke was called the Earl of Clanricarde; Fitzpatrick was given the name of the Baron of Ossory, and they returned to Ireland with their new English titles. Henry, free, open-handed, generous fellow as he was — for he was really very generous — gave them not only titles, but he gave them a vast amount of property, which happened to be stolen from the Catholic Church. He was an exceedingly generous man with other people's goods. He had a good deal of that spirit of which Artemus Ward made mention when he said he was quite content to see his wife's first cousin go to the war. In order to promote the Reformation—not Protestantism, but his own Reformation in Ireland—Henry gave to these Irish earls with their English titles, all the abbey lands, all the convents, and all the churches that lay within their possessions. The consequence was he enriched them, and to the eternal shame of the O'Neill and the O'Donnell, McWilliam Burke, and Fitzpatrick of Ossory, they had the cowardice and the weakness to accept the gifts at his hands. Then they came home with the spoils of the monasteries and their English titles. Now, mark! The Irish people were as true as steel on that day when the Irish chieftains were false to their country. Nowhere in the previous history of Ireland do we read of the clans rising against their chieftains; nowhere do we read of the O'Neill and the O'Donnell being despised by their own people, but on this occasion, when they came home, mark what follows. O'Brien, Earl of Thomond, when he arrived in Munster, found half of his dominions in revolt against him. The Burkes of Connaught, as soon as they heard that McWilliam, their natural leader—the earl—had accepted the abbey lands, the very first thing they did was to depose him and set up another man, not by the title of the Earl of Clanricarde, but by the title of McWilliam Oughter. When O'Neill, Earl of Tyrone, came home to Ulster, he was taken by his own son, clapped into jail, and died there.[16] O'Donnell, Earl of Tyrconnell, came home, and his own son and all his people rose up against him and drove him out of the midst of them.

Now, I say, in the face of all this, Mr. Froude is not justified in stating that Ireland threw the Pope overboard, for, remember, these chieftains did not renounce the Catholic religion—according to Mr. Froude they only renounced the Papal supremacy; they did not become Protestants, they only became schismatics and ceased to be Catholics, and Ireland would not stand that.

Henry died in 1547, and I verily believe that, with

all the badness of his heart, if he had lived for a few years longer his life would not have been so much a curse as a blessing to Ireland, for the simple reason that those who came after him were worse than himself. He was succeeded by his child-son, Edward VI. Edward was under the care of the Duke of Somerset. Somerset was a thoroughgoing Protestant, and did not believe in the Papal supremacy, in the Mass, in the sacraments—in anything that formed the especial teaching of the Catholic Church. He was opposed to them all, and he sent over to Ireland his orders, as soon as Henry was dead and when young Edward was proclaimed king, to put the laws in force against the Catholics. The churches were pillaged, the bishops and priests driven out, and, as Mr. Froude puts it, "the emblems of superstition were pulled down." The emblems of superstition, as Mr. Froude calls them, were the figure of Christ crucified, the statues of His Blessed Mother, and the statues and pictures of His saints. All these things were pulled down and destroyed; the crucifix was trampled under foot, and the ancient statue of our Lady of Trim was publicly burned. The churches were rifled and sacked. Then, as Mr. Froude elegantly puts it, "Ireland was taught a lesson that she must yield to the new order of things or stand by the Pope." "And Irish tradition," he says, "and ideas became inseparably linked with religion." Perfectly true, Mr. Froude! He goes on to say, in eloquent language, "Ireland chose its place on the Pope's side, and chose it irrevocably, and from that time the cause of the Catholic religion and Irish independence became inseparably one." (Great applause.) If the learned gentleman were present I have no doubt he would rise up and bow his thanks to you for the hearty manner in which you have received his sentiments. I am sure, as he is not here, he will not take it ill of me when I thank you in his name.

Edward died after a short reign, and then came Queen Mary, who is known in England by the title of "Bloody Mary." She was a Catholic, and without doubt she persecuted her Protestant subjects. But Mr. Froude makes this remark in his lecture. He says, "There was no persecution of Protestants in Ireland, because there were no Protestants there to be persecuted." He goes on to say, "those who were in the land fled when Mary came to the throne."

Now, my friends, I must take the learned historian to task in this. The insinuation is that if any Protestants had been in Ireland the Irish Catholic people would have persecuted them. The impression that he tries to leave on the mind is that we Catholics are only too glad to imbrue our hands in the blood of our fellow-citizens on the question of religious differences and of doctrine. And he goes on to confirm this impression by saying, "the Protestants who were in Ireland fled." As much as to say, whatever chance they had in England, they had no chance in Ireland.

Now, what are the historic facts? The facts are

that during the reign of Edward VI., and during the later years of his father's reign, certain apostates from the Catholic faith were sent over to Ireland as bishops—men whom even English history convicts and condemns of every crime. As soon as Mary came to the throne these gentlemen did not wait to be ordered out—they went out of their own accord. It was not a question at all of the Irish people—it was a question between the Catholic Queen of England and certain English bishops foisted upon the Irish Church. They thought it was the best of their play to clear out, and I verily believe they acted very prudently.

But, as far as regards the Irish people, I claim for my native land that they never persecuted on account of religion. I am proud in addressing an American audience to be able to lay this high claim for Ireland—that the genius of the Irish people is not a persecuting genius. There is not a people on the face of the earth so attached to the Catholic religion as the Irish race. But there is not a people on the face of the earth so unwilling to persecute or to shed blood in the cause of religion as the Irish. And here are my proofs. Mr. Froude says that the Protestants made off out of Ireland as soon as Mary came to the throne. But Sir James Ware, in his annals, tells us, that the Protestants were being persecuted in England under Mary, and actually fled over to Ireland for protection. He gives even the names of some of them. He tells us that John Harvey, Abel Ellis, John Edmunds, and Henry Haugh, all natives of Cheshire, came over to

Ireland to avoid the persecution in England. They brought a Welsh Protestant minister named Thomas Jones with them. Nay, more, these four gentlemen were received so cordially, and were welcomed so hospitably, that they actually founded highly respectable mercantile houses in Dublin. We have another magnificent proof that the Irish people are not a persecuting race. When James II. assembled his Catholic Parliament in Ireland, in 1689, the Catholics had been more than a hundred years under the lash of their Protestant fellow-citizens, robbed, plundered, imprisoned, and put to death for their conscientious adherence to the Catholic faith. At last the wheel got turned, and in 1689 the Catholics were up and the Protestants were down. That parliament assembled to the number of two hundred and twenty-eight members. The Celt, the Irish Catholic element, was in a sweeping majority. What was the first law they made? The very first law that that Catholic Parliament passed was as follows: "We hereby decree that it is the law of this land of Ireland that neither now or ever again shall any man be persecuted for his religion." This was the retaliation they took on them. Was it not magnificent? Was it not a grand specimen of that spirit of Christianity, that spirit of forgiveness and charity, without which, all the dogmatic truths that were ever revealed won't save or ennoble the Christian man?"

And now, coming to good Queen Bess, as she is called, Mr. Froude lays it on her very heavy. He speaks of her rule in language as terrific in its severity as I could, and far more, for I have not the learning or the eloquence of Mr. Froude. But he says one little thing of her worthy of remark. He says Elizabeth was reluctant to draw the sword; but when she drew it she never sheathed it until the star of freedom was fixed upon her banner, never to pale. This is a very eloquent passage. But the soul of eloquence is truth. Is it true, historically, that Elizabeth was reluctant to draw the sword? Answer it, ye Irish annals; answer it, history of Ireland. Elizabeth came to the throne in 1558. The following year, 1559, there was a parliament assembled by her order in Dublin. What do you think were the laws that were made by that parliament? It was not a Catholic Parliament, but an Anglo-Irish and Protestant Parliament. It consisted of seventy-six gentlemen. Generally speaking, the parliaments in Ireland used to have from two hundred and twenty to two hundred and thirty members. This parliament of Elizabeth consisted of seventy-six picked men. The laws that that parliament made were, first, "Any clergyman not using the 'Book of Common Prayer'—the Protestant prayer-book—or using any other form of prayer, either in public or private, the first time he is discovered, he is to be deprived of his benefice for one year and suffer imprisonment in jail for six months. For a second offence he is to forfeit his income forever, and to be put into jail, to be let out only at the queen's good pleasure, whenever she thought proper. For the third offence he was to be put in close confinement for life."

This is the lady that was reluctant to draw the sword, my friends. Remember, this was the very year after she was crowned queen. She scarcely waited a year, and yet this was the woman that was reluctant to draw the sword.

So much for the **priests, now for the** laymen. "If any layman was **discovered** using another prayer-book except Elizabeth's prayer-book—he was sent into **jail** for a year, and if caught doing this a second time, he was put into **prison for the rest of his** life." Every Sunday **the people** were obliged to **go to the** Protestant church. If any one refused to go—for **every time he refused he was fined twelve** pence. That would be about **twelve shillings of our** present **money.** And besides the fine of twelve pence, he was **to incur the** censure of the Church, whatever that meant. "The star of freedom," says Mr. Froude, "was never to pale, and the queen drew the sword in the cause of that star." But, my friends, freedom meant whatever fitted in Elizabeth's mind; freedom meant **for our fathers a** slavery, tenfold increased by the addition of persecution of the unfortunate Irish. If this **be Mr.** Froude's idea of the star of freedom, all **I can** say is the sooner such a star falls from **the firmament of** Heaven, and the world's history, the **better.**

In what state was the Irish Church? We have the authority of the Protestant historian, Leland, that there were two hundred and twenty parish churches in Meath, and in a few years' time there were only one hundred and five of them left with the roofs on. "All over the kingdom," says Leland, "the people were left without any religious worship, and under the pretext of obeying the orders of the State, they seized all the most valuable furniture of the churches, which they exposed for sale, without decency or reserve." A number of hungry adventurers were let loose upon the Irish Church and Irish people by Elizabeth. They not only robbed them, but plundered their churches, and shed the blood of the bishops, priests, and people of Ireland in torrents, as Mr. Froude himself acknowledges. He tells us "that in the second rebellion of the Geraldines, such was the state to which the fair province of Munster was reduced, that you might go through the land, from the furthermost point of Kerry until you came into the eastern plains of Tipperary, and you would not even hear as much as the whistle of the ploughboy, or behold the face of a living man. And that the trenches and ditches were full of the corpses of the people;" that "the country was reduced to a howling, desolate wilderness." The poet Spenser describes it in the most terrific and graphic style; and even he, case-hardened as he was, —being one of the plunderers and persecutors himself — acknowledges that the state of Munster was such that no man could look upon it with a dry eye. Sir Henry Sydney, one of Elizabeth's own deputies, speaks of the Irish Church. "So deformed," he says, "and overthrown a church, there is not, I am sure, in any region where the name of Christ is professed, such horrible spectacles to behold, as the burning of villages, the ruin of churches—yea, the view of the bones and skulls of the dead, who, partly by murder, partly by famine, have died in the fields, as in troth hardly any Christian with dry eyes can behold." There is the testimony of the state to which this terrible woman had reduced unhappy Ireland. Stafford, another English authority and statesman, says, "I knew it was bad, very bad, in Ireland; but that it was so stark nought I did not believe."

And in the midst of all this persecution there was still a reigning idea in the mind of the English government; it was still the old idea of rooting out and extirpating the Irish from their own land, to which was added the element of religious discord and persecution. It is evident that this was still in the mind of the English people. Elizabeth, who, Mr. Froude says, "never dispossessed an Irishman of an acre of his land," Elizabeth, during the terrible war which she had waged in the latter days of her reign against heroic Hugh O'Neill in Ulster, threw out such hints as these, "The more slaughter there is, the better it will be for my English subjects; the more land they will get." This woman, who, Mr. Froude tells us, "Never confiscated, and would never listen to the idea of the confiscation of property;" this woman, when the Geraldines were destroyed, took the whole of the vast estates of the Earl of Desmond, and gave them all quietly and calmly to certain Englishmen from Lancashire, Devonshire, Somersetshire, and Cheshire; and in the face of these truths, recorded and stamped on the world's history, I cannot understand how any man can come in and say of this atrocious woman, "Whatever she did, she intended for the good of Ireland." The annals of my own order record that there were six hundred Dominican Friars in Ireland in her time. "There are said to have been but four Fathers of the Order of St. Dominick left remaining at the time of Elizabeth's death," says Mr. McGee, in his history of Ireland. Five of our bishops received at her hands the crown of martyrdom; yet, during the half century of blood that marks her reign, we do not read of one single apostate among the bishops, and but half-a-dozen at most from all the orders of the clergy.

In 1602 she died, after reigning forty-one years, leaving Ireland, at the hour of her death, one vast slaughter-house. Munster was reduced to the state in which Spenser described it. Connaught was reduced to a wilderness through the rebellion of the Clanricardes, of the Burke family. Ulster, through the agency of Lord Mountjoy, was left the very picture of desolation. The glorious Red Hugh O'Donnell, and the magnificent Hugh O'Neill were crushed and defeated after fifteen years' war; and the consequence was that when James I. succeeded Elizabeth, he found Ireland almost a wilderness. What did he do? He quietly, at first, promised the Irish that they should keep their lands. He succeeded to the throne of England in 1603, and for four years—I must give him the credit—for four years he kept his word. In 1607, through a sham conspiracy, Hugh O'Neill and O'Donnell of Tyrconnel fled from the country, and then Sir Arthur Chichester, the agent of the English king, developed one of the most extraordinary schemes that was ever heard of in the relations between one country and another. They took the whole of the province of Ulster, every square foot of Ireland's richest and finest province, and cleared out the whole Irish population and handed it over bodily to settlers from England and Scotland. It was called the "Plantation of Ulster." They gave to the Protestant Archbishop of Armagh 43,000 acres of the finest land in Ireland; they gave to Trinity College in Dublin, 30,000 acres; they gave to the skinners, dry-salters and cordwainers, corporations and trades of London, 208,000 acres; they brought over colonies of Scotch Presbyterians and English Protestants and gave them lots of 1,000, 1,500 and 2,000 acres of land in extent, making them swear as a condition that they would not as much as employ one single Irish Catholic, or let them come near them. Thus millions of acres of the finest land in Ireland were taken at one blow from the Irish people, and they were thrust out of all their property.

Mr. Froude in his rapid historical sketch says: "But all this, of course, bred revenge." He tells us "in 1641 the Irish rose in rebellion." They did. Now he makes one statement, and with the refutation of that statement I close this lecture.

I know, my friends, to many among you these lectures must appear dry; we cannot help it; history generally is a dry subject. Mr. Froude tells us that in the rising under Sir Phelim O'Neill in 1642, there were 38,000 Protestants murdered by the Irish. Now, that is a grave charge; that is one of the most terrific things to accuse a people of, if it be not true. If it be true, all I can say is that I blush for my fathers. But if it be not true, why repeat it? why not, in the name of God, wipe it out with disdain from the record of history? Is it true? The Irish rose under Sir Phelim O'Neill; and, at that time, there was a Protestant parson in Ireland calling himself " a minister of the Word of God." He gave his account of the whole transaction in a letter to the people of England, begging of them to help their fellow-Protestants in Ireland. Here are his words: " It was the intention of the Irish to massacre all the English. On Saturday they were to disarm them, on Sunday to seize all their cattle and goods, and on Monday they were to cut all the English throats. The former they executed, the third one "—massacre—" they failed in." Petty, an English authority, tells us that there were 30,000 Protestants massacred at that time. A man by the name of May, another historian, puts it at 200,000; he thought, " in for a penny, in for a pound." But there was one honest Protestant clergyman in Ireland who examined minutely the details of the whole conspiracy and all the evils that came from it. What does he say? " I have discovered," he says—and gives as proof state papers and authentic records—" that the Irish Catholics in that rising massacred 2,100 Protestants; that other Protestants said that there were 1,600 more, and that some Irish authorities themselves say that there were 300 more, making altogether 4,000 persons." This is the massacre that Mr. Froude says—he just tosses it off as calmly as if it were Gospel—" 38,000 Protestants were massacred," that is to say, he has multiplied the original number by 10; whereas, Mr. Warner, the authority in question, actually says, " That there were 2,100," " and," he continues, " I am not willing to believe in the additional numbers that have been sent in." This is the way that history is written; this is the way that people are left under false impressions.

Now, from all we have seen of the terrible nature of the evils which fell upon Ireland in the days of Henry VIII.; in the days of Elizabeth; in the days of James I., I ask you, people of America, to set these two thoughts before your mind, contrast them, and give me a fair verdict.

Is there anything recorded in history more terrible than the persistent, undying resolution so clearly manifested by the English government, to root out, extirpate, and destroy the people of Ireland? Is there anything recorded in history more unjust than the systematic constitutional robbery of a people whom the Almighty God created in that island, to whom he gave that island, who had the aboriginal right to every inch of Irish soil?

On the other hand, can history bring forth a more magnificent spectacle than the calm, firm, united resolution with which Ireland stood in defense of her religion, and gave up all things rather than sacrifice what she conceived to be the cause of truth? Mr. Froude does not believe that it was the cause of truth. I do not blame him. Every man has a right to his religious opinions. But Ireland believed it was the cause of truth, and Ireland stood for it like one man.

I speak of all these things only historically. I do not believe in animosity. I am not a believer in bad blood. I do not believe with Mr. Froude that the question of Ireland's difficulties must ever remain without a solution. I do not give it up in despair; but this I do say, that he has no right, nor has any other man, to come before an audience of America—of America, that has never persecuted in the cause of religion; of America, that respects the rights even of the meanest citizen upon her imperial soil; and to ask that American people to sanction by their verdict the robbery and the persecution of which England was guilty.

## LECTURE III.

## IRELAND UNDER CROMWELL.

LADIES AND GENTLEMEN: We now approach, in answering Mr. Froude, to some of the most awful periods of our history; and I confess that I approach this terrific ground with sadness, and that I extremely regret that Mr. Froude should have opened up questions which oblige any Irishman to undergo the pain of heart and the anguish of spirit which the revision of this portion of our history must occasion. The learned gentleman began his third lecture by reminding his audience that he had closed his second with a reference to the rise, the progress, and the collapse of the great rebellion, which took place in Ireland in the year 1641, that is to say, somewhat more than two hundred years ago. He made but a passing allusion to that great event in our history, and that allusion, if he be reported correctly, stated simply that the Irish rebelled in 1641. This is his first statement —that it was a rebellion; secondly, that this rebellion "began in massacre and ended in ruin;" thirdly, that for nine years the Irish leaders had the destinies of their country in their own hands; and, fourthly, that these nine years were years of anarchy and slaughter. Nothing, therefore, can be more melancholy than the picture drawn by this learned gentleman of these nine years! and yet I will venture to say, and I hope I shall be able to prove, that each of these four statements is without sufficient historical foundation. My first position is that the movement of 1641 was not a rebellion; secondly, that it did not begin in massacre, although it ended in ruin; thirdly, that the Irish leaders had not the destiny of their country in their hands during these years; and, fourthly, whether they had or not, that these years were not a period of anarchy or of mutual slaughter. They were at the opening of a far more terrific period. We must discuss these questions, my friends, calmly and historically. We must look upon them rather like the antiquarian prying into the past, than with the living, warm feelings of men whose blood boils up with the remembrance of so much injustice and so much bloodshed. In order to understand this question fully and fairly, it is necessary for us to go back to the historical events of the times. I find, then, that James I., the man who "planted" Ulster—that is to say, who confiscated, utterly and entirely, six of the fairest counties in Ireland—an entire province—rooting out the aboriginal Irish Catholic inhabitants, even to a man, and giving the whole country to Scotch and English settlers of the Protestant religion, under the condition that they were not to have even as much as an Irish laborer on their grounds, but that they were to banish them away,—that this man died in 1625, and was succeeded by his unfortunate son, Charles I. When Charles came to the throne, bred up as he was in the traditions of a monarchy which Henry VIII. had rendered almost absolute, as we know; whose absolute power was still continued by Elizabeth under forms the most tyrannical; whose absolute power was continued by his own father, James I., he brought with him the most exaggerated ideas of royal privileges and royal supremacy. But during the days of his father, a new spirit had grown up in England and in Scotland. The form which Protestantism took in Scotland was the hard, uncompromising, and, I will add, cruel form of Calvinism in its most repellent aspect. The men who rose in Scotland in defense of their Presbyterian religion, rose, not against Catholics at all, but against the Episcopalian-Protestants of England. They defended what they called their Kirk, or covenant; they fought bravely, I acknowledge, for it; and they ended by establishing it as the religion of Scotland. Now, Charles I. was an Episcopalian-Protestant of the most sincere and devoted kind. The Parliament of England, in the very first year of Charles, admitted members who were very strongly tinged with Scotch Calvinism, and they at once showed a refractory spirit to their king. He demanded of them certain subsidies, and they refused him; he asserted certain sovereign rights, and they denied them. But whilst all this was going on in England, from the year 1630 to the year, let us say, 1641, what was taking place in Ireland? One province of the land had been completely confiscated by James I. Charles was in want of money for his own purposes, and his parliament refused to grant him any; and the poor, oppressed, down-trodden Catholics of Ireland imagined, naturally enough, that, the king being in difficulties, he would turn to them and perhaps lend them a little countenance, a little favor, if they proclaimed their loyalty and stood by him. Accordingly, the Lord-Lieutenant of Ireland, Lord Falkland, sincerely attached as he was to his royal master—hinted to the Catholics, and proposed to them that, as they were under the most terrific penal laws from the days of Elizabeth and of James I., if they should now petition the king, they might get certain graces or concessions granted to them. What were these graces? They simply involved permission to live in their own land, and permission to worship their God according to the dictates of their own consciences. They asked for nothing more—nothing more was promised to them. When their petition went before the king, his royal majesty of England issued a proclamation in which he declared that it was his intention and that he had pledged his word to grant to the Catholics and to the people of Ireland certain concessions or indulgences which he called by the name of "graces." No sooner, however, did the newly-founded Puritan element in England, and the parliament, that was fighting rebelliously against their king, hear that the slightest relaxation of the penal law was to be granted to the Catholics of Ireland, than they instantly rose and protested that it should not be. Charles, to his eternal disgrace, broke his word with the Catholics of Ireland after they had sent him £120,000 in acknowledgment of his bounty. More than this. It was suspected that Lord Falkland was too mild a man, too just a man to be allowed to remain as Lord-Lieutenant of Ireland, and he was recalled, and, after a short lapse, Wentworth, who was afterwards Earl of Strafford, was sent to Ireland as Lord-Lieutenant. Wentworth, on his arrival, summoned a parliament and they met in the year 1634. He told them the difficulties the king was in; he told them how his parliament in England was rebelling against him, and how he looked to his Irish subjects as loyal; and perhaps he told them that amongst Catholics loyalty is not a mere sentiment, but it is an unshaken principle, resting on conscience and assured through the church. And then he assured them that Charles, the King of England, still intended to keep his word, and to grant them their concessions or their graces. Next came the usual demand for money, and the Irish Parliament granted six subsidies of £50,000 each. Strafford wrote to the King of England congratulating him on having got so much money out of the Irish, and confessing that he had only expected subsidies of £30,000, whilst they granted subsidies of £50,000. The parliament met the following year, in 1635, and what do you think was the fulfillment of the royal promise to the Catholics of Ireland? Strafford had got the money. He did not wish to compromise his master, the king, so he took it upon himself, and fixed upon his memory the indelible shame and disgrace of breaking the word which he had pledged, and disappointing the Catholics of Ireland. Then, in 1635, the following year, the real character of this man came out, and what do you think was the measure that he proposed? He instituted a commission with the express purpose of confiscating, in addition to Ulster—that was already gone—the whole province of Connaught, so as not to leave an Irishman or a Catholic one single inch of ground in that land. This he called "The Commission of Defective Titles." They were commissioned to inquire into the title every man had to his property, and to inquire into it with the express and avowed purpose of finding a flaw in it, so that they could confiscate it to the crown of England. Now, remember how much was gone already, my friends: the whole of Ulster was confiscated by James I.; the same king had taken Longford from the O'Farrells, who owned it from time immemorial; had seized upon Wicklow and taken it from the O'Tooles and O'Byrnes; had taken the northern part of the county Wexford from the O'Cavanaghs, and Kings county from the O'Malloys. Now, with the whole of Ulster, and the better part of Leinster, in his hands, this minister of Charles comes in and institutes a commission, by which he was to obtain the whole of the province of Connaught, root out the native Irish population, expel every man who owned a rood of land in the province, and reduce them to beggary, starvation, and death. Here is a description of his plan as given by Leland, a historian who is hostile to Ireland's faith, and to Ireland's nationality. Leland thus describes the business: "His project," he says, "was nothing less than to subvert the title of every estate in every part of Connaught; a project which, when first proposed in the late reign, was received with horror and amazement, but which suited the undismayed and enterprising genius of Lord Wentworth." Accordingly, he began in the county of Roscommon, he passed from Roscommon to Sligo, then to Mayo, and then to Galway. The only way in which a title could be upset was by having a jury of twelve men to agree to their verdict as to whether the title was valid or not. Strafford began by picking his jury and packing them. The old story over again. The old policy which has been followed down to our own time, the policy of packing a perjured jury. He succeeded. He told the jury before the trials began that he expected them to find a verdict for the king, and between bribing and threatening them he got juries that found for him until he came into my own county of Galway. For the honor of old Galway be it said that as soon as this commission arrived in that county they could not find twelve jurors in the county Galway to pass a verdict to confiscate the property of their fellow-citizens. What was the result? The result was that the county

Galway jurors were called to Dublin before the Castle Chamber; every man of them was fined £4,000, and was put into prison until the fine was paid. Every inch of their property was taken from them, and the High Sheriff of the county Galway, not being a wealthy man, being fined £1,000, died in jail because he was not able to pay his fine. More than this. Not content with threatening the jury and coercing them, my Lord Strafford sent to the judges and told them they were to get four shillings in the pound for the value of every single property confiscated to the crown of England; and then he boasted publicly of it and said: "I have made the Chief Baron and the other justices attend to this business as if it were their own private concern." This is the way Ireland was ruled, and this is the kind of rule that the learned English historian comes to America to ask the honest and the upright citizens of this free country to endorse by their verdict, and thereby to make themselves accomplices in England's robbery. In the same year this Strafford instituted another tribunal in Ireland which he called "The Court of Wards." Do you know what this was? It was found that the Irish people, gentle and simple, were very unwilling to become Protestants. I have not a harsh word to say of the Protestants, but this I will say, that every high-minded Protestant in the world must admire the strength and the fidelity with which Irishmen, because of their conscience, cling to their ancient faith and forms of belief. This tribunal was instituted in order to take the heirs of Catholic gentlemen and bring them up in the Protestant religion, and it was to this Court of Wards that we owe the significant fact that some of the most ancient and the best names of Ireland—the names of men whose ancestors fought for faith and fatherland—are now Protestants, and the enemies of their Catholic fellow-subjects. It was by this, by such means as this, that the men of my own name became Protestant. There was not a drop of Protestant blood in the veins of the Dun Earl or Red Earl of Clanricarde. There was not a drop of other than Catholic blood in the veins of the heroic Burkes that fought during the long centuries that went before this time. There was no Protestant blood in the O'Briens of Munster, nor in the glorious O'Donnells and O'Neills of Ulster. Let no Protestant American citizen here imagine that I am speaking in disdain of him or of his religion. No! But as a historian I am pointing out the means—which every high-minded man must pronounce to be nefarious—by which the aristocracy of Ireland were obliged to change their religion. The Irish meantime waited, and waited in vain, for the fulfillment of the king's promise of a concession or a grace, as it was called. At length matters grew desperate between Charles and the parliament, and in the year 1640 Charles again renewed his promise to the Irish people and their parliament, which gave him four subsidies, eight thousand men, and one thousand horse, to fight against the Scots, who had rebelled against him. Earl Strafford went home rejoicing that he had got these subsidies and this body of men;

but no sooner did he arrive in England than the parliament, now in rebellion, laid hold of him, and in that same year, 1640, Strafford's head was cut off, and it would be a strange Irishman that would regret it. Meantime the people of Scotland rose in armed rebellion against their king. They marched into England, and what do you think they made by their movement? They got the full enjoyment of their religion, which was not Protestant, but Presbyterian; they got £300,000, and they got for several months £850 a day to support their army. Then they retired into their own country, having achieved the purpose for which they had rebelled. In the meantime the Catholics in Ireland were ground into the very dust. What wonder, I ask you, that, seeing that the king was afraid of his English people, although personally inclined to grant these graces—he had declared that he had wished to grant them, he had pledged his royal word to grant them, the Irish had every evidence that if the King were free he would grant them—what wonder, I say, that the Irish, seeing all this and groaning under atrocious laws, should have made an effort to right themselves. The king was not free, because the parliament and the Puritan faction in England were in rebellion. And so the Irish said, and naturally: "Our king is not free; if he were he would be just. Let us arise in the name of the king and assert our own rights." They arose like one man. Every Irishman, every Catholic in Ireland, arose on the 23d of October, 1641, with the exception of the Catholic lords of the Pale. And now I give you the reasons for this rising, as recorded in the memoirs of Lord Castlehaven, who was by no means prejudiced in favor of the Irishmen. He tells us they rose for six reasons: "First, because they were generally looked down upon as a conquered nation, seldom or never trusted like natural or free-born subjects." The old feeling still coming up, dear friends. The very first reason given by this Englishman why the Irish people rose was that the English people treated them contemptuously. Oh, when will England learn to treat her subjects or her friends with common respect?—when will that proud Anglo-Saxon haughtiness condescend to urbanity and kindness in the treatment of those around them? I said it in my first lecture, I said it in my second lecture, and I prove it in this; that it was the contempt as much as the hatred of the Englishman for the Irishman that lay at the root, and lies at the root to-day, of that bitter spirit and terrible antagonism that exist between these two nations. The second reason given by my Lord Castlehaven is that "the Irish saw that six whole counties in Ulster were escheated to the crown, and little or nothing was bestowed on the natives, but the greater part bestowed by King James on his own countrymen, the Scotch." The third reason is, that in Strafford's time the crown laid claim to the counties of Roscommon, Mayo, Galway, and Cork, and some parts of Tipperary, Limerick, Wicklow and others. The fourth reason was, that "great severities were used against Roman Catholics, which, to a people so fond of their religion as the Irish are, was no small inducement to make them, whilst there was an opportunity, stand upon their guard." The fifth reason was that " they see how the Scots, by pretending grievances and taking up arms to get them redressed, had not only gained divers privileges and immunities, but got £300,000 for their visit to England, besides £850 a day for several months together. And the last reason was that they saw a storm brewing, as the misunderstanding arose between the king and the parliament. They believed that the king would grant them anything they in reason could demand; at least more now than they could otherwise expect." Now, I ask you, were not these reasons sufficient? I appeal to the people of America, I appeal to men who know what civil and religious liberty means, for a high-spirited people whose spirit was never broken, never yielded; for a people not inferior to the Anglo-Saxon, either in gifts of intellect or in bodily energy; for a people thus forsaken, down-trodden, as our fathers were, would not one, any one, of these reasons be sufficient justification to rise? And had they not an accumulation of all those causes, which would have made them the meanest of mankind if they had not seized upon that opportunity? An English Protestant writer of the time, writing in " Howell's Hibernicus," in 1643, says, "That they had sundry grievances and grounds of complaint, both touching their estates and their consciences, which they pretended to be far greater than those of the Scotch; for they fell to think that if the Scotch were suffered to introduce a new religion, was it reason they should be punished in the exercise of their old, which they glory never to have altered." There was another reason for the revolt, my friends, and a very competent one, and it was this: Charles had the weakness and the folly, I can call it nothing else, to leave at the head of the Irish cause two Lord Justices named Sir John Borlass and Sir William Parsons. These were both ardent Puritans and partisans of the parliament; they were anxious to see the fall of the English monarch; they were his bitterest enemies, and they thought he would be embarrassed in his fight with the parliament in England by a revolution in Ireland, so the very men who were the guardians of the State lent themselves to promote the revolution by every means in their power. For instance, six months before this revolution broke out, Charles gave them notice that he had received intelligence that the Irish were going to rise; they took no notice whatever of the king's advertisement; the Lords of the Pale, who refused to join the Irish people in their uprising, appealed to the Justices in Dublin for protection, and it was refused them; they asked to be allowed in the city, that they might be saved from the incursions of the Irish, and that permission was refused them; they were forced to stay in their castles and in their houses, and the moment that any of the Irish in rebellion came near, their houses and castles were declared forfeited to the State. And so the English Catholic Lords of the Pale—the Lords of Gormanstown, Howth, Trimbleton, and many others, were actually forced by the government to join hands with the Irish, and to draw their swords in the national cause. Moreover, the Irish knew that their friends and fellow-countrymen were earning distinction and honor and glory upon all the battle-fields of Europe, in the service of Spain, France, and Austria, and they hoped in that rising that these their countrymen would help them in the hour of their need.

Accordingly, on the 23d of October, 1641, they rose. What was the first thing they did? According to Mr. Froude, the first thing they did was to massacre all the Protestants that they could lay their hands on. Well, thank God, this is not the fact. The very first thing that their leader, Sir Phelim O'Neill, did, was to issue a proclamation, on the very day of the rising, which spread through all Ireland, in which he declared: "These are to intimate and make known unto all persons whatsoever, in and through the whole country, that the true intent and meaning of us whose names are hereunto subscribed, that the first assembling of us is nowise intended against our Sovereign Lord the King, nor hurt of any of his subjects, either English or Scotch, but only for the defense and liberty of ourselves and the Irish natives of this kingdom. And we further declare, that whatsoever hurt hitherto hath been done to any person shall be speedily repaired; and we will that every person forthwith, after proclamation hereof, make their speedy repair unto their own houses under pain of death, that no further hurt be done unto any one under the like pain, and that this be proclaimed in all places. *At Dungannon*, 23 *October*, 1641.—PHELIM O'NEILL."

Did they keep this declaration of theirs? Most inviolably. I assert, in the name of history, that they did not massacre the Protestants, and I will prove it from Protestant authority. We find despatches from the Irish Government to the government in England, of the 27th of that same month, in which they gave them the account of the rising of the Irish people; there they complained, telling how the Irish stripped their Protestant fellow-citizens, took their cattle, took their houses, and took their property—but not one single word of complaint about one drop of bloodshed. And if they took their cattle and houses and property, you must remember that they only took back what was their own. A very short time afterwards the massacre began; and who began it? The Protestant Ulster settlers fled from the Irish; they brought their lives with them, at least, and they entered the town of Carrickfergus, where they found a garrison of Scotch Puritans. Now, in the confusion that arose, the poor country-people, frightened, all fled into an obscure part of the country, near Carrickfergus, to a peninsula sea called Island Magee. They were there collected for the purposes of safety to the number of more than three thousand. The very first thing these English Puritans and a Scotch garrison did, when they came together, was to steal out of Carrickfergus in the night-time go into the midst of that innocent and unarmed people, and they slaughtered man, woman and child, until they left three thousand dead behind them. And we have the authority of Leland, an English Protestant historian, who expressly says, "This was the first massacre committed in Ireland on either side." How in the name of heaven can any man so learned and, I make no doubt, so truthful as Mr. Froude—how can he, in the name of history, assert that these people began by massacring thirty-eight thousand of his fellow-countrymen—fellow-religionists, when we had in the month of December, four months after—we had a commission issued by the Lord Justice in Dublin to the Dean of Kilmore, and to seven other Protestant clergymen, to make diligent inquiry about the English and Scotch Protestants who were robbed and plundered, but not one single inquiry—not one word about all those who were murdered? The Catholics were urged into rebellion, and the Lords Justices were often heard to say that the more there were in rebellion, the more lands would be forfeited to them. "Some time before the rebellion broke out," says Carte, "Sir John Clotworthy declared, in a speech in the English House of Commons, that the conversion of the Irish Papists would only be effected by the sword in one hand and the Bible in the other, and Mr. Pym gave out that they would not leave a priest in Ireland." Sir Wm. Parsons (one of the Lord Justices) positively asserted before so many witnesses at a public entertainment that within twelve months no Catholic should be seen in Ireland. It was the old story—it was the old adage of James I:[18] "Root out the Irish; give Ireland to English Protestants and Puritans and you will regenerate the land!" Oh! from such regeneration, for my own land, or any other land or people, good Lord, deliver us! "This rebellion," says Mr. Froude, "began in massacre and ended in ruin." It ended in ruin most terribly; but if it began in massacre, Mr. Froude, you must acknowledge as historical truth that the massacre was on the part of your countrymen and your religionists. Then the war began—a war far more religious than national; for, in truth, the emancipation of Ireland from the English yoke was never contemplated nor mentioned throughout. It was an uprising of the Catholics against the sanguinary spirit of Puritanism, which openly threatened them with utter destruction. Dr. Warner tells us that it was evident, from a letter of the Lords Justices to the Earl of Leicester, the Lord Lieutenant, "that they hoped for an extirpation, not of mere Irish only, but of all the old English families that were Roman Catholic." It was a war that continued for seven years; it was a war in which the Irish chieftains had not the destinies of their nation in their own hands, as Mr. Froude asserts; but were obliged to fight, and to fight like men, in order to try and achieve a better destiny and a better future for their people. Who can say that the Irish chieftains held the destinies of Ireland in their hands during these nine years when they had to meet every successive army that came to them, inflamed with religious hatred and enmity, but animated, I must say, by a spirit of bravery of which the world has seldom seen the like? Then he adds, "That these were years of anarchy and mutual slaughter." Now let us consider the history of the event. No sooner had the English Lords of the Pale, who were all Catholics, joined the Irish, than they at once turned to the Catholic bishops who were in the land. They called them together in synod, and on the 10th of May, 1642, the bishops of Ireland, the lords of Ireland, the gentry and commoners met together and founded what is called The Confederation of Kilkenny. Amongst their numbers they selected for the supreme council, three archbishops, two bishops, four lords, and fifteen commoners. These men were to remain in permanent session, governing the country, making laws, watching over the army, and, above all, preventing cruelty, robbery, and murder. A regular government was formed, and they actually established a mint, and coined there money for the Irish nation. They established an army under Owen Roe O'Neill, who commanded the Ulster troops, Thomas Preston, who took the command in Leinster, Gerald Barry in Munster, and John Burke as Lieutenant-General for Connaught. During the first month they gained some successes. Most of the principal cities in Ireland opened their gates to them; the garrisons were carefully saved from slaughter, and the moment their opponents laid down their arms, their lives were as sacred as that of any man in the ranks of their own army. Not a drop of blood was shed by the Irish with any sort of connivance on the part of the government of the country—that is to say, the Supreme Council of Kilkenny. I defy any man to prove that there was a single act which that Supreme Council enacted, which could sanction or approve, directly or indirectly, deeds of violence. Now, after a few months of successes, the army of the Confederation experienced some reverses. The Puritan party was recruited and fortified by English armies coming in, and the command in Dublin was given to a gentleman whose name ought to be familiar to every Irishman. His name was Sir Charles Coote, and I want to read some of that gentleman's exploits to you. "Sir Charles," and mind you this is by Clarendon, no friend of Ireland, "besides plundering and burning the town of Clontarf, at that time did massacre sixteen of the towns-people, men and women, besides three suckling infants; and in that very same week fifty-six men, women and children, in the village of Bullough, being frightened at what had been done in Clontarf, went to sea to shun the fury of a party of soldiers which had come out of Dublin, under Col. Clifford, and being pursued by the soldiers in boats, they were overtaken and thrown overboard." Sir William Burliss advised the governor, Sir Charles Coote, to the burning of corn, and to give man, woman and child to the sword. Sir Arthur Loftus writes to the same purpose and same effect. An edict of the council at that time will tell you in what spirit our Protestant friends waged their wars with us: "It is resolved that it is fit that his

Lordship do endeavor" with his Majesty's forces (this was given to Earl Ormond) " to wound, kill, slay and destroy, by all the ways and means that he may, all the said rebels and their adherents and relievers, and burn, spoil, waste, consume, destroy and demolish all the places, towns, and houses where the rebels are or have been relieved or harbored, and all the hay and corn therein, and to kill and destroy all the men there inhabiting capable to bear arms. Given at the Castle of Dublin, on the 23d of February, 1641." And signed by six precious names. Listen to this: Sir Arthur Loftus, Governor of Naas, marched out with a party of horse, which was joined by another party sent from Dublin by the Marquis of Ormond, and they killed such of the Irish as they met, without stopping to inquire whether they were rebels or not. Oh, my friends! listen to this: "But the most considerable slaughter was in a great strait of furze seated on a hill where the people of several villages, taking the alarm, had sheltered themselves. Now, Sir Arthur, having invested the hill, set the furze on fire on all sides, where the people, being in considerable numbers, were all burned or killed, men, women, and children. I saw," says Castlehaven, "the bodies and the furze still burning." In the years 1641 and '42, many thousands of the poor innocent people of the county of Dublin, shunning and fearing the English soldiers, fled into the thickets and furze, which the soldiers actually fired, killing as many as endeavored to escape, or forcing them back again to be burned. And for the rest of the inhabitants, for the most part, they died of famine. Not only by land, where we read of sometimes seven thousand of our people, men, women, and children, without discrimination, being destroyed by these demons as recorded by the historian Borlase, who tells us, speaking of Sir William Coles' regiment: "Starved and famished of the vulgar sort, whose goods were seized on by this regiment, seven thousand;" but even by sea, we read that there was a law made if any Irishmen were found on board ships by his Majesty's cruisers they were to be destroyed. "The Earl of Warwick [this is in Clarendon's account] and the officers under him at sea, had, as often as he met with any Irish frigates, or such freebooters as sailed under commission, taken all the seamen who became prisoners to them of the nation of Ireland, and bound them back to back and thrown them overboard into the sea without distinction as to their condition, if they were Irish." In this cruel manner very many poor men perished daily of which the king said nothing, because his Majesty could not complain of it without being concerned in favor of the rebels in Ireland. Again, the Marquis of Ormond sent Captain Anthony Willoughby with one hundred and fifty men, who had formerly served in the fort of Galway, from thence to Bristol. The ship that carried them was taken by a Captain Swanley, who was so inhuman as to throw seventy of the soldiers overboard, under the pretense that they were Irishmen, although they had faithfully served his

Majesty against the rebels there in the time of the war. You will ask if that captain was punished for the slaughter. Here is the punishment he got. In June, 1644, we read in the journal of the English House of Commons, that Captain Swanley was called into the House and had given to him, by the English House of Commons, for his good service, a chain of gold of £200 value, and Captain Smith had another of £100 value. Sir Richard Grenville was very much esteemed by the Earl of Leicester, who was Lord Lieutenant of Ireland, and more still by the Parliament, for the signal act of cruelty he had committed upon the Irish, hanging old men who were bedridden because they would not discover where their money was, and old women, some of whom he killed after he had plundered them and found less than he had expected. In a word, they committed atrocities which I am ashamed and afraid to mention. They tossed infants taken from their mothers' bosom, upon their bayonets. Sir Charles Coote saw one of his soldiers playing with a child, throwing it into the air and then spitting it upon his bayonet, and he laughed and said he enjoyed such frolic. They brought children into the world before their time by the Cæsarian operation of the sword, and the children thus brought forth by them into misery from out of the womb of their dead mothers they immolated and sacrificed in the most cruel and terrible manner. I am afraid, I say again, afraid of your blood and mine, to tell one-tenth, aye, one-hundredth part of the cruelties that these terrible men committed upon our race.

Now I ask you to contrast with all this, the manner in which the Irish troops and the Irish people behaved. "I took Athy by storm," says Lord Castlehaven, "with all the garrison, 700 men, prisoners. I made a present of them to Cromwell, desiring him by letter that he would do the like with me, as any of mine should fall into his power. But he little valued my civility, for in a few days after he besieged Gowran, and the soldiers . . . giving up the place with the officers, he caused the Governor and some other officers to be put to death."

Sir William St. Leger, going down into Munster, seems to have slaughtered man, woman, and child, upon his march. Among others, a man named Philip Ryan, who was the principal farmer of that place, he put to death without the slightest hesitation, but some of Philip Ryan's friends and relatives retaliated somewhat on the English, and there was fear that the Catholic people would massacre all the Protestant inhabitants of the place. Now mark what follows: "All the rest of the English" (this is in Cartes' life of Ormond), "All the rest of the English were saved by the inhabitants of that place in their houses, and had the goods which they confided to them safely restored. Dr. Samuel Pullen, the Protestant Chancellor of Cashel, and the Dean of Clonfert, with his wife and children, was preserved by Father James Saul, a Jesuit. Several other Romish priests distinguished themselves on this occasion by their endeavors to save the English, particularly Father Joseph Everard, and Redmond English, both Franciscan friars, who hid some of them in their chapel, and even under their altar. The English who were thus preserved were according to their desire safely conveyed into the county of Cork, by a guard of the Irish inhabitants of Cashel. Now, my friends, the war went on from 1641 to 1649, with varying success. Cardinal Runuccini was sent over by the Pope to preside over the Supreme Council of the Confederation of Kilkenny, some time before the news came to Ireland that gladdened the nation's heart, namely, that the illustrious Owen Roe O'Neill had landed upon the coast of Ulster. This man was one of the most distinguished officers in the Spanish service, at a time when the Spanish infantry were acknowledged to be the finest troops in the world. He landed in Ireland. He organized an army, drilled them and armed them—though imperfectly—but he was a host in himself; and in the second year after his arrival he drew up his army, and met General Munro, and his English forces, at the ford of Benburb, on the Blackwater. The battle began in the morning, and raged throughout the early hours of the day, and before the evening sun had set, England's main and best army was flying in confusion, and three thousand two hundred and forty-three of their best soldiers were stretched upon the field, and choking up the ford of Benburb, whilst the Irish soldier stood triumphant upon the field which his genius and his valor had won. Partly through the treachery of Ormond and Preston, partly and mainly through the agency of the English lords, who were coquetting with the English government, the confederation began to experience the most disastrous defeats, and Ireland's cause was already broken and almost lost, when, in the year 1649, Oliver Cromwell arrived in Ireland. Mr. Froude says, and truly, that he did not come to make war with rosewater, but with the thick, warm blood of the Irish people. Mr. Froude prefaces the introduction of Oliver Cromwell to Ireland by telling us that the Lord Protector was a great friend of Ireland—a liberal-minded man that interfered with no man's liberty of conscience, and he adds that if Cromwell's policy was carried out, " in all probability I would not be here speaking to you of our differences with Ireland to-day." He adds, moreover, that Cromwell had formed a design for the pacification of Ireland, which " would have made future trouble there impossible." What was this design? Lord Macaulay tells us what this design was. Cromwell's avowed purpose was to end all difficulties in Ireland, whether they arose from the land question or from the religious question, by putting a total and entire end to the Irish race by exterminating them from the face of the earth. This was the admirable policy, my friends, in order to pacify Ireland and create peace; for the best way, and the simplest way, to keep any man quiet is by cutting his throat. The dead do not speak, the dead do not move, the dead do not trouble any one. Cromwell came to destroy the Irish race, and the Irish Catholic faith of the people; and so to put an end at once to all claims for land, and to all disputes arising out of a religious persecution. But I ask this learned gentleman, does he imagine that the people of America are either so ignorant or so wicked as to accept the monstrous proposition that the man who came into Ireland with such an avowed purpose as this, could be declared to be the friend of the real interests of the Irish people? Does he imagine there is no intelligence in America; that there is no manhood in America; that there is no love for freedom, and for life in America? and the man must be an enemy of religion and of life itself before such a man can sympathize with the blood-stained Oliver Cromwell. These words of the historian, I regret to say, sound like bitter irony and mockery in the ears of a people whose fathers Cromwell came to destroy. "But," he says, "the Lord Protector did not interfere with any man's conscience. The Irish," he says, "demanded liberty of conscience. 'I interfere with no man's conscience,' says the Lord Protector, 'but if by liberty of conscience you Catholics mean having a priest and the Mass, I can tell you you cannot have this, and you never will have it as long as the Parliament of England has power!'" Now, I ask you, what do these words mean? To grant the Catholics liberty of conscience; their consciences telling them that their first and very greatest duty is the hearing of the Mass—to grant them liberty of conscience, and then to deny them the priest and their Mass. Surely it is a contradiction in words and an insult to intelligence to propound so monstrous a proposition! "But," says Mr. Froude, "you must understand me. Of course I acknowledge the Mass to be an ancient and beautiful rite; but you must remember that in Cromwell's mind the Mass only meant a system that was shedding blood all over Europe; a system of the Church that never knew mercy, but slaughtered the people everywhere; and, therefore, he was resolved to have none of it." Ah! my friends, if the Mass was the symbol of slaughter, Oliver Cromwell would have had more sympathy with the Mass.

And so the historian seeks to justify the cruelty in Ireland against the Catholics by alleging cruelty on the part of the Catholics against their Protestant fellow-subjects in other lands. Now, this word of the historian he has repeated over and over again in many of his writings at other times and in other places, and I may as well put an end to this. Mr. Froude says: "I hold the Catholic Church accountable for all the blood that the Duke of Alva shed in the Netherlands;" and I say to Mr. Froude; I deny it. I cannot allow the Catholic Church to be made accountable for the acts of Alva or of his master, Charles V., or of any other emperor, general, or scheming politician, were he a cardinal, a bishop, or any other. I never will accept a Richelieu, a Wolsey, or a Mazzarin, as reflecting either the genius or spirit of Catholicity; and as to Charles V. and his servant Alva, we all know that they were perfectly willing to sack Rome and oppress the Pope whenever it suited their political purposes.

Alva fought in the Netherlands against subjects that rebelled against the King of Spain. Alva fought in the Netherlands against a people, the first principles of whose new religion seemed to be an uprising against authority; of the State questions the Catholic Church had nothing to say. If Alva shed the blood of the rebels, and if these rebels happened to be Protestants, there is no reason for fathering the shedding of that blood upon the Catholic Church. Mr. Froude says that the Catholic Church is answerable for the blood that was shed in the massacre of St. Bartholomew's Day under Marie de Medicis in France. I deny it. The woman who gave that order had no sympathy for the Catholic Church. It was altogether a State measure. She had France divided into factions, and she endeavored by court intrigue and villainy of her own—for a most villainous woman she was—to stifle the opposition of certain people with blood. The representations that were made in Rome were that the king's life was in terrible danger, and that that life was preserved by heaven; and Rome sang a *te deum* for the safety of the king and not for the shedding of the blood of the Huguenots. And then among these Huguenots there were Catholics who were slain because they were in the opposite division and faction. This proves that the Catholic Church was not answerable for the shedding of such blood. But, on the other hand, the blood that was shed in Ireland was shed exclusively on account of religion at this particular time; for when, in 1643, Charles I. made a treaty for a cessation of hostilities with the Irish through the confederation of Kilkenny, the English Parliament, as soon as they heard that the king had ceased hostilities for a time with their Irish patriotic fellow-subjects, at once came in and said: "September 20, 1643. It was resolved, upon the question, that this house doth hold that a present cessation of arms with the rebels in Ireland is destructive to the Protestant religion."

I regret to say, my Protestant friends, that the men of 1643, the members of the Puritan House of Parliament in England, have fastened upon that form of religion the formal argument and reason why Irish blood was to flow in torrents—lest the Protestant religion might suffer. In this day of ours we are endeavoring to put away from us all sectarian bigotry, and we deplore the faults committed by our fathers on both sides. Mr. Froude deplores the blood that was shed, and so do I. But, my friends, it is a historical question, resting upon historic fact and evidence, and I am bound to appeal to history as well as my learned antagonist, and to discriminate and put back the word which he puts out, namely, "that toleration is the genius of Protestantism." He makes this astounding assertion in his third lecture, that persecution was hostile to the genius of Protestantism. Nay, he goes further and says, speaking of the Mass, that "the Catholic Church has learned to borrow one beautiful gem from the crown of her adversary—she has learned to respect the rights of conscience in others." I wish that the learned gentleman's statement could be more fully proved by history. Oh, how much I desire that in saying these words he had spoken historic truth. No doubt he believes what he says; but I ask him, and I ask every Protestant here to-night, at what time, in what age, in what land, has Protestantism ever been in the ascendant without persecuting th Catholics who were around them? I say it not in bitterness, but I say it simply as historic truth. I cannot find in the records of history during these ages up to a few years ago any time when Protestants in Ireland, in Sweden, in Germany, or anywhere else, gave the slightest toleration, or even permission to live when they could take life from their Catholic fellow-subjects. Even to-day where is the strongest spirit of religious persecution? Is in not in Protestant Sweden? Is it not in Protestant Denmark? Who to-day are persecuting, I ask you? Is it Catholics? No! but Protestant Bismarck in Germany.

All this I say with regret and shame. I am not only a Catholic, but a priest; not only a priest, but a monk; not only a monk, but a Dominican monk; and from out of the depths of my soul I repel and repudiate the principle of religious persecution for any cause, in any land. Oliver, the apostle of blessings to Ireland, landed in 1649. He besieged Drogheda, defended by Sir Arthur Aston and by a brave garrison, and when he had breached the walls, when they found their position was no longer tenable, they asked, in the military language of the day, that they would be spared and quarter given. That quarter was promised to all the men who ceased fighting and laid down their arms. "All the officers and soldiers of Cromwell's army promised quarter to such as should lay down their arms, and performed it as long as the place held out; which encouraged others to yield" *(Carte)*. "The soldiers threw down their arms upon a general offer of quarter" *(Clarendon)*. "Quarter was offered and accepted" *(Lingard)*. The promise was observed until the town was taken. When the town was in his hands, Oliver Cromwell gave orders to his army for an indiscriminate massacre of the garrison, and of every man, woman, and child of that large city. The people, when they saw the soldiers slain around them, when they saw the men killed on every side, when they saw the streets of Drogheda flowing with blood for five days, fled, to the number of a thousand of aged men, and women, and children, and they took refuge in the great church of St. Peter, in Drogheda. Oliver Cromwell drew his army around that church, and out of that church he never allowed one of these thousand innocent people to escape alive. He then proceeded to Wexford, and there a certain commander of the garrison, named Stafford, admitted him into the city, and he massacred the people there again. Three hundred of the women of Wexford, with their little children, gathered around the great market cross, in the public square of the city; for they thought in their hearts, all terrible as he was, that he would respect and save those who were under the sign of man's redemption, that he would spare all those who were under the image of the rood. Oh, how vain the thought! Three hundred poor defenseless women screaming for mercy under the cross of Jesus Christ, and Cromwell and his barbarous demons around them. He destroyed them, so as not to let one of those innocents escape until his men were ankle deep in the blood of the women of Wexford. He retired from Ireland after having glutted himself with the blood of the people. He retired from Ireland, but he wound up his war by taking 80,000 and some say 100,000, and driving them down to the southern ports of Munster. He shipped 80,000 at the least calculation to the sugar plantations of Barbadoes, there to work as slaves, and in six years' time such was the treatment they received there, that out of the 80,000 there were not twenty men left. He collected 6,000 Irish boys, fair, beautiful, stripling youths, and he put them in ships and sent them also off to Barbadoes, there to languish and to die before they ever came to the fullness of their age, and of their manhood. Oh, great God! is this the man? is *this* the man who has an apologist in the learned, frank, generous, and gentlemanly historian, who comes, in oily words, to tell the American people that Cromwell was one of the bravest men that ever lived, and one of the best friends that Ireland ever had? Now we must pass on. Oliver died in 1658. Here I meet a singular assertion of Mr. Froude's, who tells us that much as he regrets all the blood that was shed by a terrible vengeance, still it resulted in great good for Ireland. And the good consisted in this: the Parliament, after Cromwell's victories, found themselves masters of Ireland, and the Irish people lying in blood and ruin before them—what was their next measure? Their next measure was to pass a law driving all the people of Ireland who owned any portion of the land, all the Irish landowners and the Catholics out of Ulster, Munster and Leinster. On the 1st of May, 1654, all Ireland was driven across the Shannon into Connaught. The phrase used by the Cromwellians on the occasion was "That they were to go to hell or Connaught." The solemnity of the historic occasion which brings us together will not permit me to make any remarks on such a phrase as this; however, the Irish did not go to hell, but they were obliged to go to Connaught. Lest, however, they might have any relief come to them by sea, lest they might even enjoy the sight of the fair provinces and the fair land which was once their own, he made a law that no Irishman transplanted into Connaught was to come within four miles of the river Shannon on the one side, or within four miles of the sea on the other side. There was a cordon of English soldiery and English forts drawn about them, and there they were to live in the bogs, in the fastnesses and in the wild wastes of the most desolate region in Ireland; there they were to pine and expire by famine and by every form of suffering that their Heavenly Father might permit to fall upon them.

Then we read that numbers of Englishmen came

over to Ireland, and I don't blame them! The fair plains of Munster were there desolate, waiting for them; the splendid valleys of Leinster, with their green bosoms, were waiting for the hand to put in the plough, or put the spade into the bountiful earth. They were waiting for an owner; so the English came over, and they were very glad to get this fair land of Ireland for almost nothing. Cromwell settled down his troops there. Those rough Puritan soldiers, who came to Ireland with the Bible in one hand and the sword in the other, took possession of the country, and, according to Mr. Froude, here is the benefit that resulted from Cromwell's plantation. In fifteen years they changed Ireland into a garden; all the bogs were drained, all the fields were fenced, all the meadows were mown, all the fallow fields were ploughed, and the country was smiling; never was there anything so fine seen before in Ireland, as the state of things brought about by Cromwell. The poor Irish peasantry that were harassed by the priests, bishops, and chieftains now enjoyed comfort, peace, and quiet, as the servants of the new English owners and possessors of the soil. Well! I wish for Ireland's sake that this picture were true.

And this fifteen years of which Mr. Froude speaks must have begun in 1653; because it was only in September of that year that the English Parliament declared that the war was over in Ireland. Up to that time there was war and bloodshed. Now there was peace. Oh, my friends! he made it a solitude; he made it a desert, and called it peace. But was it a peaceful desert?

Oliver Cromwell died in 1658, and now I want to read for you the state of Ireland—Mr. Froude's "Garden"—at that time. Ireland, in the language of Scripture, now laid void as a wilderness; five-sixths of her people had perished—men, women and children were found daily perishing in ditches, starved. The bodies of many wandering orphans, whose fathers had embarked for Spain, and whose mothers had died of famine, were fed upon by wolves. In the years 1652 and '53, the plague and famine had swept away the inhabitants of whole counties, so that a man might travel twenty or thirty miles and not see a living creature—man, beast, or bird; they were all dead, or had quit these desolate places. The troopers would tell stories of places where they saw smoke; it was so rare to see fire or smoke, either by day or night. In two or three cabins where they went, they found none but aged men, with women and children, and, in the words of the prophet, "they became as a bottle in the smoke;" their skin was black, like an oven, because of the terrible famine; they were seen to eat filthy carrion out of the ditch, black and rotten, and were said to have even taken corpses out of the graves to eat. A party of horse, hunting for Tories on a dark night, discovered a light and thought it was a fire which the Tories used. They made fires in those waste countries to cook their food and warm themselves. Drawing near, they saw it was a ruined cabin, and posting themselves around they peeped in at the windows, and there they saw a great fire of wood, and sitting around it was a company of miserable women and children, and between them and the fire a dead corpse lay broiling, which, as the fire roasted, they cut and ate.

A year before Oliver died, in 1657, we find a member of the Irish Parliament, Major Morgan, declaring that the whole land of Ireland was in ruin, for beside the cost of rebuilding the churches and court-houses and market-houses, which were very heavy, they were under a very heavy charge for public rewards paid for the destruction of three burdensome beasts. What do you think the three beasts were? The wolf, the priest, and the tory. Now let me explain the state of the "garden" to you. During these years of which Mr. Froude speaks so flatteringly, there was actually a grant of land issued within nine miles of the City of Dublin, on the north side, that is to say, on the most cultivated side of the city, under conditions of keeping a pack of wolf-hounds to hunt and destroy the wolves. The wolves increased in Ireland from the desolate state of the country; they fed on the dead carcasses of men and beasts; they increased in Ireland so that they actually came famished to the very gates of Dublin, and had to be driven away. Does this look like a garden? Is this the kingdom of peace and plenty, and comfort, and happiness into which the Irish peasant had come at last—where everything was peace and security, where the bogs were all drained and the fields beautifully fenced by the dear Cromwellians who got possession of the land? When the relics of the army were embarking for Spain, some of the soldiers had magnificent Irish wolf-dogs, and wished to take their dogs with them. They were stopped at the port, and the dogs taken from them for the purpose of hunting the wolves that infested the country.

This is my first answer to Mr. Froude's assertion that Ireland was a garden. The second beast mentioned by Major Morgan in the Irish House of Commons was—the priest. And he was to be hunted down like the wolf. There were five pounds set upon the head of a dog-wolf, and there were five pounds set on the head of a priest, and ten pounds on the head of a bishop or a Jesuit. Mr. Froude says that these severe laws were not put into execution. He tells us that whilst parliament passed these laws they privately instructed the magistrates not to execute them. So merciful, so tolerant, is the genius of Mr. Froude's Protestantism! We have however the terrible fact before us that the English Parliament made laws commanding the magistrates, under heavy fine and penalties, to execute these laws. We find the country filled with informers, we find priest-hunting actually reduced to a profession in Ireland, and we find strange enough, the Portuguese Jews coming all the way from Portugal in order to hunt priests in Ireland, so valuable was the privilege regarded. In 1698, under William III., there were in Ireland four hundred and ninety-five religious and eight hundred and seventy-two secular priests, and in that **very year, out of** four hundred and ninety-five friars, four hundred and twenty-four were shipped off from Ireland into banishment and into slavery; and of the eight hundred and odd secular priests that remained in the land, not one of them would be allowed to say Mass in public or private, nor indeed remain in the country until he first took the oath to renounce the supremacy of the Pope —of Papal abjuration—in other words, until he became a Protestant. It is all very well for my learned friend to tell us that the laws were not put into execution; but what is the meaning of such entries as these?—"Five pounds on the certificate of Major Thomas Stanley"—"to Thomas Gregson, Evan Powell and Samuel Ally, being three soldiers in Colonel Abbott's dragoons, for arresting a popish priest named Donogh Haggerty, taken and now secured in the county jail of Clonmel, and the money," it says, "to be equally divided between them." "To Arthur Spunner, Robert Pearce and John Bruen, five pounds, to be divided equally between them, for their good service performed in apprehending and bringing before the Right Honorable Lord Chief Justice Pepys, on the 21st of January, one popish priest named Edwin Dinn." "To Lieutenant Edward Wood, on the certificate of Wm. St. George, Esq., justice of the peace, county Cavan, twenty-five pounds, for five priests and friars apprehended by him, namely, Thomas McKernan, Turlough O'Gowan, Hugh McGowan, Torlogh Fitzsimmons, who on examination confessed themselves to be priests and friars." "To Sergeant Humphrey Gibbs"—a nice name—" and to Corporal Thomas Hill, of Colonel Lee's company, ten pounds, for apprehending two popish priests, namely, Maurice Prendergast and Edward Fahy, who were secured in the jail of Waterford and afterwards were transported to foreign parts."

In 1655 a general arrest of priests by the justices of the peace was ordered, under which, in April, 1656, the prisons in every part of Ireland seem to have been filled to overflowing. On the 3d of May, the governors of the respective precincts were ordered to send them with sufficient guards from garrison to garrison to Carrickfergus, to be there put on board such ship as should sail with the first opportunity for Barbadoes.

The third burdensome beast was "the tory." The great aim of the English government was to give security to the English and Scotch planters. For this end, 40,000 of the fighting men of Ireland were forced to abandon wives and children, and embark for Spain. The deserted families, the few remaining landed proprietors with their tenants and their wives, sons and daughters, were forced into Connaught. The aboriginal Irish and the old English were involved in a common ruin, and we read how Lord Roche of Fermoy, reduced in his old age to beggary, was forced with his daughters to go on foot into Connaught, there to end his days in misery in some wretched cabin, whilst his ancient inheritance was divided between a troop of hungry, canting hypocrites of Cromwell's army. The land was filled with such unfortunates. Inspired by such sights, bands of desperate men formed themselves into bodies, under the leadership of some dispossessed gentleman, who had retired into the wilds on the surrender of the army to which he belonged, or who had "run out" again after submitting, and resumed arms rather than transplant into Connaught. He soon found associates and followers, who, being beggared, were desperate as himself. These were the Tories, and the country was soon infested with them. The great regions left waste by war and transplantations gave them scopes for harboring in, and the inadequate numbers of the forces of the Commonwealth to fully control so extensive a country as Ireland, left them at liberty to plan their surprises. If Ireland was the garden that Mr. Froude describes it to be, how comes it to pass, that no Cromwellian settler throughout the length and breadth of the land dared to take a piece of land unless there was a garrison of soldiers within his immediate neighborhood? Nay, even under the very eyes of this garrison of Timolin, in Meath, the Tories came down, robbed, plundered, set fire and destroyed the homesteads of certain English Cromwellian settlers, for which all the people of the neighborhood, of Irish names and of Irish parentage, were at once taken and banished out of the country. In a word, the outlaws, who thirty years afterwards appeared as Rapparees, who are described to us in such fearful terms by the English historian, continued to infest and desolate the country, and we find accounts of them in the State Papers down to the latter year of the reign of George IV. And this was the garden! This was the land of peace, of comfort, and of plenty!

Now, my friends, came the restoration in 1659. Charles II. was restored to the throne of England. Well, the Irish had been fighting for his father; the Irish had bled and suffered fighting his enemies, and they were now banished into Connaught; they naturally expected that when the rightful heir to the throne would come into his inheritance they would be recalled and put into their estates. They might have expected more. They might have expected to be rewarded by honors, titles and wealth. But what is the fact? The fact is, that Charles II., at the restoration, left nearly the whole of Ireland in the hands of the Cromwellian settlers, and by an act of settlement secured them in their estates, leaving the property and the wealth of the country to the men who had brought his father to the scaffold, and leaving in beggary, destitution and in ruin, the brave and loyal men who had fought for him and his house. At first, indeed, there was a Court of Claims opened; for, remember, in England, no sooner had Charles come to the throne than all the Cromwellian settlers who had taken the property of the English royalists were at once put out, and the English lords and gentlemen got back their property and estates. Not so in Ireland. The Court of Claims was opened in the first year of the reign of Charles. As soon as it was perceived that the Irish Catholic gentlemen began to claim their property they shut up the court at once. Three thousand of these claims remained unheard. As Leland says, "The people of Ireland were denied the justice which is given to the commonest criminal—the justice of having a fair and impartial hearing." Nugent, afterwards Lord Riverstone, writes at this time, "There are in Ireland to-day 5,000 men who never were outlawed, and yet who have been put out of their estates, and now by law can never recover their estates again." More than this; no sooner is Charles seated on the throne of England than the Irish Parliament began to afflict the already down-trodden people of Ireland by a legislation the most infamous that can be imagined. In 1673 the English Parliament furiously demanded of the king to expel all the Catholic bishops and priests from Ireland, and to prohibit the Papists from living there without a license. In order to appease the Protestant plunderers, Charles, against his conscience and against his royal gratitude, obeyed them. Law after law was passed in that year and the succeeding years abolishing and destroying, as far as they could, every vestige of the Catholic religion in Ireland. Mr. Froude here again makes the astounding assertion that when the restoration came, the Catholic religion and the Catholic people came back with it. He tells us that the Catholic Archbishop of Dublin was received in state at Dublin Castle. What are the facts? The Primate, Edmund O'Riley, was banished. Peter Talbot, the Archbishop of Dublin, although he was in a dying state, got leave but a short time before to return to

Ireland that he might die in the land of his birth. He was arrested in Maynooth, near Dublin, and shut up in a dungeon, and there he died a miserable death of martyrdom.

We find at this very time a reward offered of ten pounds for any one who would discover an officer of the army attending at "Mass"—five pounds for a trooper, and four shillings for a private soldier, who was discovered to have heard "Mass." Oliver Plunket, the holy primate of Armagh, was seized by Lord Ormond, in 1679. They knew that they could not condemn him of any lawlessness or treason in Ireland, and they brought him over to London, packed an English jury to try him, and they murdered him at Tyburn, on the 1st of July, 1681.

It is true these penal laws were somewhat relaxed for some years before Charles the Second's death. That event took place in 1685, and James II. came to the throne. Three years afterwards William of Orange landed to dispute with him the title to the crown of England. Now, although James II. was a Catholic he was the lawful King of England, and that no man will deny. William was married to James's daughter Mary, and William came to England with an army of 15,000 men at his back; he came to inquire who was the lawful heir to the crown. Well! James fled to France as soon as William landed with his army. Mr. Froude says "that he abdicated when he fled to France." I deny that James abdicated. When he retired for a time from the face of his enemy, he called upon his subjects both in England and Ireland to stand to their king like loyal men. The English betrayed him; the Irish rose up again for the Stuart king, and declared they were loyal men, and they would stand by their monarch. James came to Ireland in 1689, and summoned a parliament, the same parliament which Mr. Froude speaks of in his lecture as a persecuting parliament; he says that "they attainted almost every single Protestant proprietor in Ireland by name; that they did this lest any one should escape out of their net." Now, what are the facts of that parliament of 1689? The very first thing that they declared, although they had suffered more than any other people of religious persecution, the very first law they made was, " that there should be no more religious persecution in Ireland, and that no man from that day forward should suffer for his conscience or his faith." It is perfectly true, that they passed a bill of attainder, but they passed that bill not against Protestants, but against every man of the land that was in arms against King James—whom they recognized as their king—every man who refused to obey him and his government. I ask you, in doing that, did they not do their duty? Did they not do precisely what is always done in time of rebellion? England was in rebellion against James, its lawful king. James was in Ireland and there was an Irish Parliament with James at its head, declaring every man was an outlaw who was in arms against him. Against these outlaws the Bill of Attainder was passed—this persecuting measure of which Mr. Froude speaks when he mentions this parliament.

William came to Ireland and opened the campaign in 1690. Mr. Froude says in his description of this "that William brought with him a motley army, ill-disciplined and dissolute, but that the Irish were never so strong, never were so well drilled, or so perfectly equipped as they were at the time." Now, here are the proofs as given by history: "William's army consisted at first of 45,000 veteran soldiers, a motley assemblage, it is true, of various nationalities, but well trained and most of them veteran troops; all were well armed and equipped in the best possible manner. They were supplied with everything requisite for war and more especially with a numerous train of artillery. The Irish army of James numbered 23,000 imperfectly disciplined troops, wanting in nearly everything necessary for a campaign." This we have on the evidence of the Duke of Berwick; he was serving in the army at the time. At the Battle of the Boyne, Mr. Froude says "that the Irish did not make even a creditable stand," and I regret, bitterly regret, that the learned gentleman should have forgotten himself so far as to have ventured in the faintest whisper to impute a want of courage to the soldiers of the Irish race. At the Battle of the Boyne, James and his army were on the south bank of the river. William with his army advanced down from the north. William's muster-roll of the army on that morning shows the figures of 51,000 men. James's army had not increased from the original 23,000. William was a lion-hearted and brave soldier. James, I regret to say, had forgotten the tradition of that ancient courage and gallantry which distinguished him as Duke of York—when he was Lord High Admiral of England. The one had the heart of a lion, the other that of a stag. The Irish fixed upon James an opprobrious name in the Irish language, which on an occasion like this I will not permit myself to repeat. On the morning of the Battle of the Boyne, William detached 10,000 men, who went up the stream some miles to ford it near the hill of Slane. James could scarcely be prevailed upon to send one or two regiments to oppose the 10,000 men with their artillery headed by Count Schombers. The evening before the battle James sent away six guns towards Dublin. How many do you think remained? Only six pieces of artillery remained with the Irish army on that day. How many were opposed to them? We have it on historic record that William brought into the field on the day of the Battle of the Boyne, fifty heavy pieces of artillery, and four mortars. Then he advanced and crossed the river. These Irish troops, of which Mr. Froude says that they did not make even a respectable stand, were out-generaled that day; they had at their head a timorous king who had already sent away his artillery and his baggage; who had already drawn around his person, two miles away, all the best disciplined of the French soldiers, and only the raw levies—all the young Irishmen—were opposed to the fifty-one thousand of the bravest men of Europe. Well! they crossed the Boyne, and the Duke of Berwick is my authority for stating this. He says, "With admirable courage and gallantry the Irish troops charged the English ten times after they had crossed the river." Ten times! these poor young fellows, with no generals, charged upon the English with a dash as brave as that with which O'Brien, Lord Clare, swept down upon them at Fontenoy. Ten distinct times did they dash against the terrible lines of William's veterans, and then they retreated like an army in perfect order at the command of their superior officers. The Irish, according to the Duke of Berwick, lost one thousand men in killed and wounded. The English, according to Story, who was present, lost four hundred men killed, which would make, according to the usual proportion, a total loss of twelve per cent. killed and wounded. Thus it appears that the Irish gave more than they got. Now came the first siege of Athlone. That same year, 1690, the English army advanced on the line of the Shannon. "At Athlone," Mr. Froude says, "the Irish deserted posts which they easily might have made impregnable." Now, what are the facts? At the first siege Col. Richard Grace beat back the English under Douglas, although the latter had an army of twelve thousand men, twelve cannon and two mortars.

Then William advanced upon Limerick; he brought with him the whole strength of his army. He had, when he went to Limerick, thirty-eight thousand effective men in regular line of battle. In the town of Limerick there was the army of James, made up partly of Irish under the immortal Sarsfield, and partly of French under a general named Lauzun. The whole force amounted to about twenty thousand infantry only, one-half of which was armed, and three thousand five hundred cavalry encamped five miles outside the city. When the great English army with its king was approaching the city the French general, seeing it so defenseless, actually left the town with the troops, swearing that "the town could be taken with roasted apples." Sarsfield with the Irish remained. William advanced before the town and battered it with his cannons until he made a breach thirty-six feet wide, and then assaulted it with twelve thousand of his picked men. They actually entered the town, and were beaten out of the walls of Limerick; beaten back over the broken ruins. The very women of Limerick entered into the contest, fighting side by side with their brothers, husbands and fathers. After four hours, however, of fighting, William Prince of Orange withdrew from the assault and left two thousand men in the breaches of Limerick; two thousand men and one hundred and fifty-eight officers were destroyed in that assault. The next day King William sent a message to the city asking them for leave to bury his dead. And the answer he got was—"Begone! We will give you no leave. Take yourself away, and we will bury your dead." In the second siege of Athlone of the following year the English town was occupied by Colonel

Fitzgerald. St. Ruth, with the Irish army, lay two miles away on the other side of the Shannon. The English town was assailed by eight thousand men against the four hundred commanded by Fitzgerald. The Irish troops who remained under Fitzgerald stopped the whole English army, and fought until out of the four hundred men not two hundred were left before they crossed the bridge that goes to the other portion of the town. Before they crossed the bridge they broke one of the arches. The English army with all their artillery battered that Irish town until they did not leave a house or stone upon stone in it. After the Irish troops retired, the English attempted to plank over the broken arch of the bridge. They had their guns fixed to sweep the bridge. Eleven Irish soldiers came out to take the planks off; and out of the eleven, such was the fierce, sweeping fire of the English artillery, only two escaped. Again the English advanced to the attack, and again eleven other Irish sergeants of the various regiments came out, in the face of the whole English army, and of their artillery, and deliberately, under their very eyes, destroyed the wooden bridge they were making over the Shannon. And when the town was taken at last, it was a mere heap of ruins. It was taken not from any want of bravery on the part of the Irish soldiers, but through the folly and misguided conduct of the French general, St. Ruth, who refused to succor them.

Of Aughrim I will not speak; because, my friends, Mr. Froude himself acknowledges that at Aughrim the

Irish soldiers fought bravely. And because I have for this English gentleman, really and truly, a sincere regard and esteem, I would ask him to do what I myself would do if I was in his position; I would ask him to reconsider the word in which he seems to imply a taint of cowardice on Irishmen at home and abroad, and in the name of God to take that word back; because that word will remain and breed bad blood for many a day. In 1691, the second siege of Limerick began, and so gallant was the resistance, so brave the defense, that William of Orange, who was a brave man—and if left to himself, would have been a tolerant and mild man—who bore no ill-will to the Irish, being a stranger to them, and only in Ireland simply to further the service of war—who saw in the Irish a high-spirited and brave people, was obliged to come to terms, and the city capitulated. In the capitulation, Sarsfield signed for the Irish; they received honorable terms from the royalty of England. By those very articles, as citizens and as Catholics, their rights were recognized to every liberty of conscience and of religion. Scarcely was the treaty of Limerick signed by the Lords Justices, than a French fleet entered the Shannon. A French fleet of eighteen ships of the line, with twenty transports, three thousand men, two hundred officers, and, above all, ten thousand stand of arms, with clothing and provisions. They came! but they came too late for Sarsfield and for Ireland, Sarsfield had surrendered. He might have taken back that word; he might have broken these articles, with the French forces and fleet at his back. But Sarsfield, to his honor, was an Irishman—and he was far too honorable a man to violate the treaty of Limerick which he had signed with his gallant hand. Would to God that the honor of Sarsfield had also been in the hearts of the other men who, on the part of England, signed that treaty! No! the Lords Justices went back to Dublin with the treaty signed, with the honor of the royalty of England committed to it, and the next Sunday after they arrived in Dublin they went to Christ Church Cathedral to perform their devotions, and the sermon was preached by Dopping, the Lord Bishop of Meath. Now, I am more or less a professional preacher, and I have a certain *esprit de corps*. I have the feeling for preachers that every man has for his own profession. I like to see them uphold the honor of their profession. What do you think was the sermon that Dopping preached? He preached—and I am ashamed to say it, although it is true he was a Protestant Bishop—" on the sin of and the sinfulness of keeping your oath or faith with a Papist." Immediately after the articles of Limerick were signed, we have the testimony of Harris, the historian of William III., who says: " The justices of the peace and sheriffs and other magistrates, presuming on their power in the country, did in an illegal manner dispossess several of their majesty's subjects, not only of their goods and chattels, but of their lands and tenements, to the great disturbance of the peace of the kingdom, and to the reproach of the law and their majesty's government." We find those Lords Justices themselves complaining, in a letter of the 19th November, six weeks after the treaty was signed, that their lordships had received complaints from all parts of the land of the ill-treatment of the people who had submitted to their majesty's protection and were included in the articles of that treaty. And the consequence was, that actually the men who had previously refused to embark with Sarsfield to go to Spain and France with him, came back in thousands, back to the English Government to obtain leave to join Sarsfield in exile; to let them go to fight the battles of France, Spain, and Austria, because there was no room in Ireland for a Catholic Irishman nor even for an honest man.

Now began a time the most lamentable for Ireland. William himself was anxious to keep his royal word, and would have kept it if they had allowed him. But the same pressure was put upon him as was brought to bear on Charles I. The Irish Protestant faction would not allow the Catholics to live in the land. The English Parliament would not allow a Catholic to breathe in the land; and William was coerced to comply with their request, and a series of the most terrible laws that can be imagined were passed in the very teeth of the articles signed in Limerick. Three years after the siege of Limerick, the parliament were urged by the grievances of the Protestants of Ireland—the poor fellows complained "that the Catholics would not give them leave to live!" They poured in their petitions to the House of Commons. We find a petition from the Protestant mayor and aldermen of the city of Limerick; complaining, in their own words, "that they were greatly damaged in their trade by the great number of Papists residing there;" also praying to be relieved of them. We find the coal-porters of Dublin sending in a petition to parliament, and it was as follows: A petition of one Edward Sprag—another nice name!—and others, in behalf of themselves and other Protestant porters in and about the city of Dublin, complaining that one Darby Ryan, a Papist, actually employed porters of his own religion, and the petition was entertained by the Irish House of Commons and sent to the "Committee on Grievances." The parliament passed an act for the better securing of the government against the Papists; and the first act of that parliament was that no Catholic in Ireland was to be allowed to have a gun, pistol, or sword of any kind, or weapon of offense or defense. The consequence of disobeying this law was banishment or fine and imprisonment, at the discretion of the court, or else the pillory, or whipping. Now, here are the reflections of Mr. Mitchel: "It is impossible to describe the minute and curious tyranny to which this statute gave rise in every parish of the island; especially in districts where there was an armed yeomanry, exclusively Protestant, it fared ill with any Catholic who fell for any reason under the displeasure of his formidable neighbors. Any pretext was sufficient for pointing him out to suspicion. Any neighboring magistrate might visit him at any hour of the night, and search his bed for arms. No Papist was safe from suspicion who had any money to pay in fines, and woe to the Papist who had a handsome daughter."

The second act that they passed was for the purpose of brutalizing the Irish Catholic people by ignorance. They made a law that no Catholic was to send his son to a Catholic school or to a Catholic teacher. No Catholic child was to be sent out of Ireland to receive a Catholic education elsewhere; or if any parent or guardian was found sending money, clothing or any thing else to a Catholic child in a Catholic school, there was forfeiture, imprisonment, and fine; disabilities of various kinds, but above all the old and favorite punishment, forfeiture of estate.

The third act passed was: "That all Popish archbishops, bishops, vicars-general, Jesuits, monks, friars, or other regular Popish clergy or Papists, exercising any ecclesiastical jurisdiction, were ordered to depart out of the kingdom before the 1st of May, 1698. If any remained after that day, or if any returned, the delinquents were to be transported; if they returned again, they were guilty of high treason, to suffer accordingly" —that is to say: to be hanged, drawn and quartered.

You would imagine now, at least, that the Papists were down as far as they could be put down. You would imagine now, at least, that the Protestant religion was safe in Ireland. Ah! my friends, William was succeeded by his sister-in-law, Queen Anne. She was a Stuart—the daughter of James II., for whom

Ireland shed its blood; the granddaughter of Charles I., for whom Ireland had shed its blood; and one would think she would have some heart—some feeling for that people. Here is the way she showed it:

A parliament under this good queen passed a law to further prevent the growth of Popery. What a strange plant this Popery must be! They had been chopping it up, and cutting it down, tramping it under foot, blowing it up with gunpowder, digging out the roots, as if they thought that would extirpate it. Yet, year after year, a parliament comes in and says: "We must stop the growth of Popery;" and passed laws to stop the growth of Popery. By the first Act of this parliament of good Queen Anne, it was enacted, that if a son of a Papist should ever become Protestant, his father might not sell, or mortgage his estate, or dispose of it, or any portion of it, by sale. The Protestant son became master of his father's estate; or if any child, no matter how young, conformed to the Protestant religion, it reduced his father at once to be a tenant for life, and the child was to be taken from the father, and placed under the guardianship of some Protestant relative. They made a Papist incapable of purchasing any landed estates, or rents, or profits arising out of land, or hold any lease of lives, or any other lease exceeding thirty-one years.

Finally, they capped the climax, by passing a law, that no Papist or Catholic was to have a horse worth more than five pounds. If he had one worth five thousand pounds, and a Protestant came up to offer him five pounds for the horse, whether he took the offered money or not, the Protestant was at liberty to seize the Catholic's property. In a word, every enactment that could degrade, vilify, or annihilate the people, was the order of the day, and the business of parliament, from the days of Elizabeth, down to the days when America burst her chains, and before her terrible presence England grew afraid of her life, and began to relax her penal laws. I feel, my friends, that I have detained you too long, upon a subject, which, indeed, was dreary and desolate ground to travel over. I for my part never would have invited the citizens of America, or my fellow-countrymen, to enter upon such a desolate waste; to renew in my heart and yours so deep and terrible a sore, if Mr. Froude had not compelled me to lift the veil, and to show you the treatment our fathers received at the hands of England. I do it, not at all to excite national animosity—not at all to stir up bad blood. I am one of those most willing to say, " Let bygones be bygones; let the dead bury their dead." But if any man—I care not who he be—how great his reputation—how grand his name, in any walk or line of science or history; if any man dare to come—as long as I live—to say that England's treatment of Ireland was just, and was necessary—was such as can receive the verdict of an honest man, or of a nation or a people—if any man dare say that, either at home or abroad, Irishmen have ever shown the white feather in the hour of danger—if I was on my death-bed, I would rise to contradict him.

## LECTURE IV.

## GRATTAN AND THE VOLUNTEERS.

LADIES AND GENTLEMEN:—I have perceived in the public papers that Mr. Froude seems to be somewhat irritated by remarks that have been made as to his accuracy as a historian. Lest any word of mine might hurt in the least degree the just susceptibilities of an honorable man, I beg beforehand to say that nothing was further from my thoughts than the slightest word, either of personality or disrespect for one who has won for himself so high a name as an English historian. And therefore I sincerely hope, that it is not any word which may have fallen from me, even in the heat of our amicable controversy, that can have given the least offense to that gentleman. Just as I would expect to receive from him, or from any other learned and educated man, the treatment which one gentleman is supposed to show to another, so do I also wish to give to him that treatment.

And now, my friends, we come to the matter in hand. Last evening I had to traverse a great portion of my country's history in reviewing the statements of the English historian, and I was obliged to leave almost untouched one portion of the sad story—namely, the period which covers the reign of Queen Anne. This estimable lady, of whom history records the unwomanly vice of an overfondness for eating, came to the English throne on the demise of William of Orange in 1702, and on that throne she sat until 1714. As I before remarked, it was perhaps natural that the Irish people—the Catholics of Ireland, trodden into the very dust—that they would have expected some quarter from the daughter of the man for whom they had shed their blood, and from the granddaughter of the other Stuart king for whom they had fought with so much bravery in 1649. The return that the Irish people got from this good lady was quite of another kind from what they might have expected. Not content with the atrocious laws that had been already enacted against the Catholics of Ireland; not content with the flagrant breach of the articles of Limerick, of which her royal brother-in-law William was guilty, no sooner does Anne come to the throne and send the Duke of Ormond as Lord Lieutenant to Ireland, than the English ascendency, that is to say the parliament faction in Ireland, got upon their knees to the new Lord Lieutenant to beg of him, for the sake of the Lord, to save them from these desperate Roman Catholics. Great God! A people robbed, persecuted, and slain, until only a miserable remnant of them were left, without a voice in the nation's councils, without a vote even at the humblest board that sat to transact the meanest parochial business—these were the men against whom the strong Protestant ascendency of Ireland made their complaint in 1703. And so well were these complaints heard, my friends, that we find edict after edict going out, declaring that no Papist shall be allowed to inherit or possess land, or to buy land, or to have it even under a lease; declaring that if a Catholic child wished to become Protestant, that instantly that child became the owner and the master of his father's estate, and his father remained only his pensioner or tenant for life upon the bounty of his own apostate son; declaring that if a child, no matter how young, even an infant, conformed and became Protestant, that moment that child was to be removed from the guardianship and custody of the father and was to be handed over to some Protestant relation. Every enactment that the misguided ingenuity of the tyrannical mind of man could suggest was adopted and put in force. "One might indeed suppose," says Mr. Mitchell, "that Popery had been already sufficiently discouraged, seeing that the bishops and regular clergy had been banished, that Catholics were excluded by law from all honorable or lucrative employments, carefully disarmed, and plundered of almost every acre of their ancient inheritance. But enough had not yet been done to make the Protestant interest feel secure," consequently other laws were made, and clauses were added by this good Queen Anne declaring that "no papist or Catholic could live in a walled town," especially in the towns of Limerick or Galway; that no Catholic could even enter the suburbs of the town. They were obliged to remain outside of the town as if they were lepers, whose presence would contaminate and degrade their sleek and pampered Protestant fellow-citizens in the land. The persecution went on. In 1711 we find them enacting new laws, and later on, to the very last day of Queen Anne's reign, we find them enacting their laws, hounding on the magistrates and the police of the country and the informers, offering them bribes and premiums to execute these atrocious laws, and to hunt the Catholic people and the Catholic priests of Ireland as if they were fierce, untamable wolves. And, my friends, Mr. Froude justifies all this on two grounds. Not a single word has he of compassion for the people who were thus treated; not a single word has he of manly protest against the shedding of that people's blood by unjust persecution—as well as their robbery by legal enactments. But he says there were two reasons which, in his mind, seemed to justify the atrocious action of the English government. The first of these was that, after all, these laws were only retaliation upon the Catholics of Ireland for the dreadful persecutions that were suffered by the Huguenots, or Protestants, of France; and he says that the Protestants of Ireland were only following the example of King Louis XIV., who revoked the Edict of Nantes.

I could not explain this matter better than by quoting the words of the illustrious Irishman who is in the midst of us, John Mitchel.

"The recall of the Edict of Nantes, which edict had secured toleration for Protestantism in France, is bitterly dwelt upon by English writers as the heaviest reproach which weighs on the memory of King Louis XIV. The recall of the edict had taken place in 1685, only a few years before the passage of this Irish 'Act to prevent the further growth of Popery.' The differences between the two transactions are mainly these two: *first*, that the French Protestants had not been guaranteed their civil and religious rights by any treaty, as the Irish Catholics thought they held theirs, by the Treaty of Limerick; *second*, that the penalties denounced against French Protestants by the *recalling* edict bore entirely upon their religious service itself, and were truly intended to induce and force the Huguenots to become Catholics; there being no confiscations except in cases of relapse, and in cases of quitting the kingdom; but there was nothing of all the complicated machinery above described, for beggaring one portion of the population, and giving its spoils to the other part. We may add, that the penalties and disabilities in France lasted a much shorter time than in Ireland; and that French Protestants were restored to perfect civil and religious equality with their countrymen, in every respect, forty years before the 'Catholic Relief Act' purported to emancipate the Irish Catholics, who are not, indeed, emancipated yet."

Side by side with this foolish act of Louis XIV. of France, we find the Irish people ruined, beggared, persecuted, and hunted to the death, and the English historian comes and says, "Oh, we were only serving you as your people and your own fellow-religionists in France were serving us." The other reason which Mr. Froude gives to justify these persecutions was that the Irish Catholics were in favor of the Pretender —that is to say, of the son of James II., and consequently were hostile to the government. Now, to that statement I can give, I think, a most emphatic denial. The Irish Catholics had had quite enough of the Stuarts; they had shed quite enough of their blood for that treacherous and shameless race; they had no interest whatever in the succession, nor cared they one iota whether the Elector of Hanover or the son of James Stuart succeeded to the throne of England. For well they knew whether it was Hanoverian or Stuart that ruled in England, the faction at home in Ireland and the prejudices of the English people would make him, whoever he was, a tyrant over them and over their nation. And thus the persecution went on, and law after law was passed to make perfect the beggary and the ruin of the Irish people, until at length Ireland was reduced to such a state of misery that the very name of Irishman was a reproach. Under pressure of those crushing laws, a small number of the glorious race had the weakness to change their faith and to deny the religion of their fathers. The name of an Irishman was a reproach. My friends, Dean Swift was born in Ireland. Dean Swift is looked upon as a patriotic Irishman. Yet Dean Swift said that he no more considered himself an Irishman, because he happened to be born in Ireland, than an Englishman chancing to be born in Calcutta would consider himself a Hindoo. Of the degradation of the Irish and their utter prostration he went so far as to say, he would not think of taking them into account on any matter of importance any more than he would of consulting the swine. Lord Macaulay gloats over the state of the Catholics in Ireland then, and Mr. Froude views, perhaps not without some complacency, their misery. Lord Macaulay calls them pariahs, and compares their position in the disputes between the English and Irish Parliament with that of "the red Indians in the dispute between Old England and New England about the Stamp Act." And we find Bowes, the Lord Chancellor, laying down the law quite coolly and calmly, and saying that "in the eye of the law no Catholic existed in Ireland." Chief Justice Robinson made a similar declaration. Here are the words of his lordship the Chief Justice: "It appears" he says, "plain that the law does not suppose any such person to exist as an Irish Roman Catholic." Mr. Froude says that they favored the Pretender, at the very time when the government itself was attributing the quietude of the people in Ireland, not to their prostration, not to their ruin, as was the real case, but to their devoted loyalty to the crown of England. The Irish people were quite indifferent about the Pretender. They received at the time some doubtful praise for their loyalty to the House of Hanover. But, as Mr. Mitchel truly says, " If they took no part in the insurrections of 1715 and 1745, it may be said (in their favor, not to their dishonor) that it was on account of exhaustion and impotence, not on account of loyalty. If they had been capable at that time of attachment to the Protestant succession, and of loyalty to the House of Hanover, they would have been even more degraded than they actually were." As a curious instance of the utter ruin of the old race, and the shame which attached even to the name of Irishman, we have at this time an Irishman of the name of Phelim O'Neill, one of the glorious old line of Tyrone, one in whose veins flowed the blood of the great and the heroic Red Hugh, who purpled the Blackwater, who struck the Saxon at the Yellow Ford, and purpled the stream of the Blackwater with his blood. One in whose veins flowed the perhaps still nobler blood of the immortal Owen Roe O'Neill, the glorious victor of Benburb. And this good Phelim O'Neill changed his religion and became Protestant. But it seemed to him a strange and unnatural thing that a man of the name of O'Neill should be a Protestant; so he changed his name from Phelim O'Neill and called himself Felix Neal. There has been a good deal said lately about the pronunciation of proper names and what they rhyme with. This man made his name rhyme with eel—the slippery eel. Now, on this change of the gentleman's name and religion, an old parish priest wrote some Latin verses, which were translated by Clarence Mangan. I will read them, just to let you see how things were in Ireland at that time:

> All things has Felix changed. He changed his name,
> Yea, in himself he is no more the same.
> Scorning to spend his days where he was reared,
> To drag out life among the vulgar herd,
> And trudge his way through bogs in bracks and brogues,
> He changed his creed and joined the Saxon rogues
> By whom his sires were robbed, and laid aside
> The arms they bore for centuries with pride—
> The "ship," the "salmon," and the famed "Red Hand"—
> And blushed when called O'Neill in his own land.
> Poor paltry skulker from thy noble race!
> *Infelix* Felix, weep for thy disgrace!

But, my friends, the English ascendency, or the Protestant ascendency in Ireland, if you will, seeing now that they had got every penal law that they could ask for, seemed to look upon the Irish race as exterminated. This extermination in truth they had nearly accomplished, for they had driven them into the wilds and wastes of Connaught, and they would have destroyed them all, only that the work was too great, and that there was a certain something in the old blood, in the old race, that terrified them when they approached it. They had so far subdued the Catholics that they thought now, at last, that their hands were free, and nothing remained for them but to make

Ireland, as Mr. Froude says, a garden. They were to have every indulgence and every privilege. Accordingly they set to work. They had their own parliament. No Catholic could come near them or come into their towns—they were forbidden to show themselves at all. The Protestant ascendency, however, were greatly surprised to find that now that the Catholics were crushed into the earth, England began to regard the Cromwellians themselves with fear and hatred. What! They, the sons of the Puritans! They, the brave men that had slaughtered so many of the Irish and of the Catholic religion! Are they to be treated harshly? Was their trade, or their commerce, or their parliament to be interfered with? Ah! now, indeed, Mr. Froude finds tears, and weeps them over the injustice and over the folly of England, because England interfered with the commerce and with the trade of the Protestant ascendency in Ireland. These Protestant tradesmen were first-class woolen weavers; at last, the cloth they made became the very best, and took the very highest prices in all the markets of Europe, because the wool of the Irish sheep was so fine. The English Parliament made a law that the Irish traders were not to be allowed to sell any more cloth; they were not to go into any more markets to rival their English fellow-merchants. They were to stay at home; they had the island, and they might make the most of it; but no freedom in trade, nothing that would enrich Ireland—that the English Parliament forbade. Now, Mr. Froude assigns as the reason for this legislation, that England at that time happened to be under the control of a paltry lot of selfish money-jobbers and merchants. Mere accident, according to him; an accident, he confesses, which so discontented the Orange faction in Ireland that many hundreds of them emigrated and came over to America to settle in the New England States. Thither, he tells us, they carried their hatred with them, and that feeling which helped break up the British Empire. I have another theory of this great question. I hold that it was no accident of the hour at all that made England place her restrictive laws on the Irish commerce and trade. I hold that it was the settled policy of England. These men who were now in the ascendency in Ireland imagined that because they had ruined and beggared the ancient race and the men of the ancient faith, therefore they were friends, and would be regarded as friends by England. I hold it was at that time, and, in a great measure, is to-day, the fixed policy of England to keep Ireland down, to be hostile to Ireland, no matter who lives in it, whether he be Catholic or Protestant, whether he be Norman, Cromwellian, or Celt. "Your fathers," says Curran, speaking to the men of his time, a hundred years afterwards, "your ancestors thought themselves the oppressors of their fellow-subjects; but they were only their jailers; and the justice of Providence would have been frustrated if their own slavery had not been the punishment for their baseness and their folly." That slavery came, and it fell on commerce. The Protestant inhabitants of Ireland, the Protestant traders of Ireland, the planters, and the sons of the planters, were beggared by the hostile legislation of England, simply because they were now in Ireland, and had an interest in the Irish soil, and in the welfare of the country. The inimitable Swift, speaking on this subject, makes use of the following quaint fable of Ovid. He says, "The fable which Ovid relates of Arachne and Pallas is to this purpose: The goddess had heard of a certain Arachne—a virgin famed for spinning and weaving. They both met upon a trial of skill, and Pallas, finding herself almost equalled in her own art, stung with rage and envy, knocked her rival down, turned her into a spider, enjoining her to spin and weave forever out of her own bowels, and in a very narrow compass. I confess," the Dean goes on, "that from a boy I always pitied poor Arachne, and never could heartily love the goddess, on account of so cruel and unjust a sentence, which, however, is fully executed upon us by England, with the further addition of rigor and severity, for the greatest part of our bowels and vitals is extracted, without allowing us the liberty of spinning or weaving them." Thus he writes of this strange piece of legislation, which Mr. Froude acknowledges. The Irish wool was famous, and the English were outbid for it by the French manufacturers. The French were willing to give more money for a pound of Irish wool, and the English passed a law that the Irish people, the farmers, could not sell their wool anywhere but in England; so they fixed their price on it, and they took the wool, made cloth, and, as the Dean says, poor Ireland—Arachne—had to give her bowels without the pleasure of spinning or weaving. Then the Dean goes on to say, "The Scriptures tell us that oppression makes the wise man mad, therefore, the reason that some men in Ireland are not mad, is because they are not wise men." However, it were to be wished that oppression would in time teach a little wisdom to fools. Well, we call Dean Swift a patriot. How little did he think, great man as he was, of the oppression, compared with which the restriction upon the wool was nothing, the oppression that beggared and ruined a whole people, that drove them from their land, that drove them from every pleasure in life, that drove them from their country, that maddened them to desperation, and all because they had Irish names, Irish blood, and because they would not give up the faith which their consciences told them was true. And now, my friends, Mr. Froude, having related how these unjust restrictive laws forced the Protestant operatives to come to America, tries to enlist the sympathies of the American people in their behalf. If he stopped there I would not have a word to say to the learned historian. When an Englishman claims the sympathy of this or any other land for men of his people and of his religion, if they are deserving of that sympathy, I, an Irishman, am always ready and the first to grant it to them with all my heart. And, therefore, I do not find the slightest fault with this learned Englishman when he challenges the sympathy of America for the Orangemen of Ireland and the Protestants who came to this country. If these men were deserving of American sympathy, why not let them have it? But whilst Mr. Froude claims sympathy for the Protestant emigrants from Ireland, as staunch republicans and lovers of American liberty, he tells us that the Catholics of Ireland, on the other hand, were clamoring at the foot of the throne, telling King George III. that they would be only too happy to go out at his command to shoot the American people in his cause. Is that statement true or not? My friends, the learned gentleman quoted a petition presented in 1775, the very year America began to assert her independence. In that petition he states that Lord Fingal and several other Catholic noblemen of Ireland, speaking in the name of the Irish people, pronounced the American revolution an unnatural rebellion, and manifested their desire to go out and devote themselves for the best of king's, to the suppression of American liberty. First of all I ask, when, at any time in our history, has any one of these Catholic lords been authorized to speak in the name of the Irish people? But, not doubting Mr. Froude's word at all, and only anxious to satisfy myself by historic research, I have looked for this petition. I have found, indeed, a petition in Curry's collection—a petition signed by Lord Fingal and by a number of other Catholic Irishmen, addressed to his Majesty the King, in which they protest their loyalty in terms of slavish and servile adulation, but in that petition I have not been able to discover one single word about the American Revolution, not a single word of address to the king about a desire to destroy the liberties of America. Not one word! I have sought, and my friends have sought, in the records and in every document that was at our hands, for this petition of which Mr. Froude speaks, and I could not find it. There must be a mistake somewhere or other. It is strange that a petition of so much importance would not be published amongst the documents of the time. We know that Sir John Blacquiere was secretary to the Lord Lieutenant of Ireland, in 1775. Naturally enough the petition would go to him, not to rest with him, but to be presented to the king. And yet, I think I may state with certainty that the only petition that was presented to the king in 1775 was the one of which I speak, and in which there was not a single word about America or the American Revolution. But the learned historian's resources are so much more ample than mine; his resources of time, of preparation, and of talent; his resources in the varied sources of information amongst which he has lived and passed his years, that no doubt he will be able to explain this.

The Catholics of Ireland were down in the dust; the Catholics of Ireland had no voice; they had not as much as a vote for a parish beadle, much less for a Member of Parliament. Does Mr. Froude mean to tell the American people that these unfortunate wretches would not have welcomed the cry that came from across the Atlantic; the cry of a people who rose like a giant, yet only an infant in age, proclaiming the eternal liberty of men and of nations, and proclaiming that no people upon the earth should be taxed without representation, and giving the first blow, right across the face of England, that the old tyrant had received for many a year—a blow before which England reeled, and came to her knees? Does he mean to tell you or me, citizens of America, that such an event as this would be distasteful to the poor Irish Catholics of Ireland? It is true that they had crushed them as far as they could, but they had not taken all the manhood out of them. Deep and earnest was the sympathy of Catholic Ireland with America, and many a proof of her love did ancient Erin give the great young country. Lord Howe, the English general, in that year of 1775, writes home to his government in England from America, and says: "Send me out German troops." You know England was in the habit of employing Hessians. I don't say this with the slightest feeling of disrespect. I have the deepest respect for the great German element in this country; but in these times, we know that the troops of small German states were hired out by their princes to whoever took them, and engaged them to fight their battles. "Send me out German troops," he says, "for I have a great dislike for the Catholic soldiers, as they are not at all to be depended upon." They sent out four thousand troops from Ireland; but listen to this. Arthur Lee was agent of the American government in 1777, and he says, writing to Washington, "The resources of our enemy, that is to say, England, are almost annihilated in Germany, and their last resort is to the Roman Catholics of Ireland; they have already experienced their unwillingness to go, every man of a regiment raised there last year having obliged them to ship him off tied and bound." When the Irish Catholic soldiers heard that they were to go to America to cut the throats of the American people, and to scalp them, they swore they never would do it; and they had to take them, tie them, and carry them on board the ships. But Arthur Lee goes on to say, "And most certainly they will desert more than any other troops whatsoever." Louden, a historian of the time, tells us that the war against America was not very popular, even in England. "But in Ireland," he says, "the people assumed the cause of America through sympathy."

Let us leave Ireland, and go to America. Let us see how the great men who were building up the magnificent edifice of their country's freedom, laying the foundation in their own best blood, in those days—how they regarded the Irish? In 1790, the immortal George Washington received an address from the Catholics of America, signed by Bishop Carroll, of Maryland, and many others. Replying to that address, the calm, magnificent man makes use of these words: "I hope," he says, "ever to see America amongst the foremost nations in examples of justice and liberality, and I presume that your fellow-citizens will not forget the patriotic part which you took in the accomplishment of their revolution, and in the establishment of their government; or the important assistance they received from a nation in which the Roman Catholic religion is professed." In the month of December, 1781, the Friendly Sons of St. Patrick, in Philadelphia, elected George Washington a member of their society. These Friendly Sons of St. Patrick were great friends of the great American Father of his Country. When his army lay at Valley Forge, twenty-seven members of this society of the Friendly Sons subscribed between them, in July, 1780, £103,500 sterling, of Pennsylvania currency, for the American troops, who were in want of means. George Washington accepts the fellowship of their society, and he says: "I accept with singular pleasure the ensign of so worthy a fraternity as that of the Sons of St. Patrick, in this city—a society distinguished for the firm adherence of its members to the glorious cause in which we are embarked." During that time what greater honor could have been bestowed by Washington than that which he bestowed upon the Irish? When the traitor Arnold betrayed the cause at West Point, Washington was obliged to choose the very best and most reliable soldiers in his army, and send them to West Point, to take the place that was so well-nigh being betrayed by the traitor. From his whole army he selected the celebrated Pennsylvania Line, as they were called, and these men were mainly made up of Irishmen. Nay, more, not merely of Protestant Irishmen, or Northern men, or of those who, in that time, were called Scotch Irish, for that was the name which, in the year of the Revolution, designated Mr. Froude's friends, who emigrated from Ulster. But, looking over the muster-roll of the Pennsylvania Line, we find such names as Duffy, Maguire, and O'Brien; these and such as these are the names not of Palatines nor of Scotch planters in Ireland, but they are the names of thoroughbred Irish Celts. They fought and bled for Washington, and Washington loved them. And now, I wish to give you a little incident of that celebrated corps, to let you see how their hearts were in relation to America. "During the American Revolution," says Mr. Carey, "a band of Irishmen were embodied in the defense of the country of their adoption, against the country of their birth; they formed the major part of the celebrated Pennsylvania Line; they bravely fought and bled for the United States; many of these sealed their attachment with their lives; their adopted country neglected them somewhat, the wealthy, independent, and the luxurious, for whom they fought, were now rioting in the superfluities of life, while the defenders were literally half starved, half naked, their shoeless feet marked with blood their tracks upon the highways. They long bore their grievances patiently; they had long murmured; they remonstrated, imploring the necessaries of life, but in vain; a deaf ear was turned to their complaints: they felt indignant at the cold neglect and ingratitude of the country for which thousands of their companions in arms had expired on the crimson field of battle; they held arms in their hands, and they mutinied."

Well, as soon as the English commanders had heard that the Irish soldiers had mutinied, what did they do? Intelligence was carried to the British camp, and it overspread joy and gladness, that Lord Howe hoped that the period had arrived for the end of this rebellion, as it was termed, and that there was a glorious opportunity to crush out the embryo Republic. He counted much on the natural resentment of the natives of the Emerald Isle. He knew how irritable their tempers were; he calculated upon diminishing the strength and numbers of the rebels, by an accession of the same numbers to the royal army. Messengers were dispatched to the mutineers, and they had a *carte blanche* to make their own terms; promises were to be made to them if the prodigal children feeding upon husks should return to the plentiful fields of their royal masters. Liberality itself presided in their offers of abundant supplies, and provisions ample enough for their hearts' content; all arrears of pay, and pardon for past offences, were offered to them. There was not, however, any hesitation amongst these poor, neglected warriors. They refused to renounce poverty, nakedness, and ingratitude. Splendid temptations were held out to them in vain; there was no Judas, there were no Arnolds amongst them. They seized upon their tempters and trampled upon their shining gold. They sent them to their generals, and these miserable wretches paid their forfeited lives for attempting to seduce a band of forlorn, deserted, but illustrious heroes. "We prate," he says, "about the old Roman and Grecian patriotism

One-half of it is false, and in the other half there is nothing that excels these noble traits in our army; which are worthy of the pencil of a West, or a Trumbull." Mark how it is that America regarded them! mark the testimony of some of America's greatest men! Mr. Froude seems to think that the American people looked upon the Irish nation and the Irish people as represented in their great contest by the Protestant emigrants from Ireland. Was this the view that America and her statesmen took of them? No! Here is the testimony of George Washington Parke Custis, the adopted son of George Washington. The Irish, in 1829, won Catholic Emancipation; and before that time, when they were struggling for emancipation, they appealed for sympathy and moral support to America; and now this is how this great American gentleman speaks of them: "And why is this imposing appeal made to our sympathies? It is an appeal from that very Ireland, whose generous sons, alike in the days of our gloom and of our glory, shared in our misfortunes and joined in our success; who, with undaunted courage breasted the storm which once, threatening to overwhelm us, howled with fearful and desolating fury through this now happy land; who, with aspirations deep and fervent for our cause, whether under the walls of the Castle of Dublin, in the shock of our liberty's battles, or in the feeble and expiring accents of famine and misery, amidst the horrors of the prison, ship, cried from their hearts, "God save America! Tell me not," he goes on to say, "tell me not of the aid which we received from another European nation, in the struggle for independence; that aid was most, nay, all essential, to our ultimate success; but remember, years of the conflict had rolled away." The capture of Burgoyne had ratified the Declaration of Independence—the renowned combats of the Heights of Charleston and Fort Moultrie; the bloody and disastrous days of Long Island, of Brandywine, and Germantown; the glories of Trenton, Princeton, and Monmouth, all had occurred; and the rank grass had grown over the grave of many a poor Irishman who had died for America, ere the Flag of the Lilies floated on the field by the Star Spangled Banner. "But," he adds, " of the operatives in war—I mean the soldiers—up to the coming of the French, Ireland had furnished in the ratio of one hundred for one of any foreign nation whatever." Then this generous American gentleman, to whom Ireland appealed for sympathy—for Mr. Froude's is not the first appeal that has been made to the people of America—this high-minded gentleman goes on to say, " Then honored be the old good service of the sons of Erin, in the War of Independence. Let the shamrock be entwined with the laurels of the revolution; and truth and justice, guiding the pen of history, inscribe on the tablets of America's remembrance, Eternal Gratitude to Irishmen!" Remember that this was Washington's son; remember that he tells us that the old gray-headed, crippled veterans, who had fought under his father's banner in that war of independence, were accustomed to come to his house, and there he would receive them at his door, and bring them in; and he tells us affectionately of one old Irishman who had fought in the wars; who, after drinking the health of the gentleman who had entertained him, lifted up his aged eyes, and with tears he said, "Now let me drink to General Washington, who is in Heaven this day." He says on the same occasion, "Americans, recall to your mind the recollections of the heroic time when Irishmen were our friends, and when in the whole world we hadn't a friend besides. Look to the period that tried men's souls, and you will find that the sons of Erin rushed to our ranks, and, amid the clash of steel, on many a memorable day, many a John Byrne was not idle." Remember, he does not say many a Spraggs, or many a Gibbs, or men that came over with Cromwell, but—honest John Byrne. Who was this honest John Byrne of whom he speaks? He was an Irish soldier of Washington's, who, taken prisoner by the English and put on board a prison-ship, was left in chains in whe hold of the ship, pestilence being on board. He was more than half starved; he was scarcely able, when he was called on deck, to crawl like a poor, stricken creature to the commander's feet to hear what sentence was to be pronounced upon him. And when the English commander offered him liberty, life, clothing, food, and money, if he would give up the cause in which he was taken prisoner and join the ranks of the British army; with a voice scarcely able to speak; raising a hand scarcely able to lift itself up, the Irishman looked to Heaven, and cried out, "Hurrah for America!" In the face of such facts, in the face of such testimony, in the presence of the honored name and record of George Washington, testifying to what the Irish Catholic men have done for America, Mr. Froude speaks as faintly as if he were speaking to the hurricane that sweeps over the ocean, when he tries to impress the American mind and the American people with any prejudice against the poor Catholics of Ireland. Speaking in the year 1809, when America was preparing for her second war with England, MacNevin records that "One of the offences charged upon the Irish, and amongst the many pretexts for refusing redress to the Catholics of Ireland, was that sixteen thousand of them fought on the side of America." But he adds "that many more thousands are ready to maintain the Declaration of Independence, and that will be their second offence."

Now, my friends, there are other testimonies as well as these of the men of the time; we have the testimony of American literary gentlemen, such, for instance, as that of Mr. Paulding. Here are the words of that distinguished gentleman: "The history of Ireland's unhappy connection with England exhibits, from first to last, a detail of the most persevering, galling, grinding, insulting, and systematic oppression to be found anywhere, except among the *helots* of Sparta. There is not a national feeling that has not been insulted and trodden under foot, or a national right that has not been withheld, until fear forced it from the grasp of England, or a dear or ancient prejudice that has not been violated, in that abused country. As Christians, the people of Ireland have been denied, under penalties and disqualifications, the exercise of the rites of the Catholic religion, venerable for its antiquity, admirable for its unity, and consecrated in the belief of some of the best men that ever breathed. As men they have been deprived of the common rights of British subjects, under the pretext that they were incapable of enjoying them, for which pretext they had no other foundation than their resistance of oppression, only the more severe by being sanctioned by the laws. England first denied them the means of improvement, and then insulted them with the imputation of barbarism." Another distinguished American, Mr. Johnson, says: "There is no instance, even in the Ten Persecutions, of such severity as that which has been exercised over the Catholics of Ireland." Thus think and thus speak the men whose names are bright in the records of literary America. Take, again, the unanimous address agreed to by the several members of the Legislature of Maryland. Speaking of Ireland, these American senators and legislators say, "This dependency of Great Britain has languished under an oppression long reprobated by all humanity, and discountenanced by all just policy. It would argue a penury of human feelings, an ignorance of human rights, to submit patiently. In the lapse of centuries which have witnessed the struggles of Ireland, but only with partial success, rebellion and insurrection have continued, with but short intervals of tranquillity. America has opened her arms to the oppressed of all nations. No people have availed themselves of the asylum with more alacrity or in greater numbers than the Irish. High is the meed of praise, rich is the reward that Irishmen have merited through the gratitude of America: as heroes and statesmen they honor their adopted country." Until such words as these are wiped out of the records of American history, until the generous sentiments which inspired them have ceased to be a portion of the American nature, and not until then, will Mr. Froude get the verdict which he seeks from America to-day. I have looked through the American archives and I have found that the foundation of these sympathies lay in the simple fact that the Catholics of Ireland were heart and soul with you, American gentlemen, with you and your fathers in that glorious struggle. I find in the third volume of the American archives a letter from Ireland, dated September 17, 1775, to a friend in New York, in which the American gentleman writing, says: "Most of the people here wish well to the cause in which you are engaged. They are raising recruits throughout this kingdom. (*The men are told that they are only going to Edinburgh to learn military discipline and then to return.*) Before they got a single Irishman to enlist they had to tell him a lie, well knowing that if he thought they were going to arm him and to send him to America to fight against the American people, he would never enter the ranks of the British army for any such purpose. A certain Major Roche went down to Cork to recruit men for America, and he made a great speech to them; it was very laughable. He called upon them as Irishmen, by all that they held sacred, the glorious nationality to which they belonged, the splendid monarch that governed them, and then he held up the golden guineas and the pound notes before them—and here is the record of the affair in the third volume of the American archives: "An account of the success of Major Roche in raising recruits to fight against America. The service was so disagreeable to the people of Ireland in general, that few of the recruiting officers could prevail upon a man to enlist and fight against their American brethren." That same year, in the British House of Commons, Mr. Johnson says: "I maintain that the sense of the best and the wisest men in the country are on the side of the Americans, and in Ireland three to one are on the side of the Americans." In the House of Lords, in the same year, of '75, the Duke of Richmond makes this statement: "Attempts have been made to enlist the Irish Roman Catholics, but the minister knows well that these attempts have been proved unsuccessful." We find again the Congress of America addressed the people of Ireland in that memorable year of 1775, and here are the words that America's first Congress sends over the Atlantic waves to the afflicted, down-trodden Irish: "Accept our most grateful acknowledgment for the friendly disposition you have always shown towards us. We know that you are not without your grievances; we sympathize with you in your distress, and we are pleased to find that the design of subjugating us has persuaded the administration to dispense to Ireland some vagrant rays of ministerial sunshine. Even the tender mercies of the government have long been cruel towards you. In the rich pastures of Ireland many hungry parasites are fed, and grow strong to labor in her destruction." We find such words as these addressed, not to the Palatines and planters; for if the Congress of America was addressing the planters and Cromwellians in Ireland, they would not have used such language as this: "In the rich pastures of Ireland many hungry parasites are fed, and grow strong to labor in its destruction."

Benjamin Franklin, of glorious and immortal name, was in Versailles, as minister from the American government. He writes to the people of Ireland in October, 1778, and says: " The misery and distress which your ill-fated country has been so frequently exposed to and has so often experienced, by such a combination of rapine, treachery, and violence as would have disgraced the name of government in the most arbitrary country in the world, has most sincerely affected your friends in America, and has engaged the most serious attention of Congress." Now I come to another honored name, that of Gulian C. Verplanck. When the Catholic Emancipation Act was passed, there was a banquet in the City of New York to celebrate the event, and this distinguished American gentleman proposed a health or a toast, and it was a Catholic toast: "The Penal Laws—*Requiescat in pace*—may they rest in peace."

"And yet," says Mr. Verplanck, "I have a good word to say for them." What was that good word? Here it is: "That in the glorious struggle for our independence, and in our more recent contest for national rights, those laws gave the American flag the support of hundreds and thousands of brave hearts and strong arms, at the same time contributing an equal portion of intellectual and moral powers."

Let us come down to our time, passing over the magnificent testimony of Henry Clay, and his sympathies for Catholic Ireland. America, even at this hour, is mourning over the grave of a great man. But a few days ago the nation accompanied to his last resting-place William H. Seward. And this illustrious American statesman said, in 1847, "Ireland not only sympathized profoundly with the trans-Atlantic colonists in their complaints of usurpation, under which she suffered more sorely than they; but, with inherent benevolence and ardor, she yielded at once to the sway of the great American idea of universal emancipation. The bitter memory of a stream of ages lifted up her thoughts, and she was ready to follow to the war for the rights of human nature, 'the propitious God, who seemed to lead the way.'"

Finally, one extract and I have done with this portion of my lecture. I find that such were the relations between Ireland and America in that struggle, that a certain Captain Wicks, of the ship *Reprisal,* in the summer of 1776 captured three prizes near the West Indies, which were English property. He detailed some of his own men on board of them, and sent them to the nearest port to be adjudged as prizes. Shortly after he came across another vessel, and he let her go, finding she was Irish property. The Marquis Chasteloux, a distinguished Frenchman who was in America in 1782, writes thus: "An Irishman, the instant he sets his foot on American soil, becomes *ipso facto* an American. This was uniformly the case during the whole of the late war." Remember, this Frenchman was fighting for you. "While Englishmen and Scotchmen were treated with jealousy and distrust, even with the best recommendations of zeal and attachment to the cause, the native of Ireland stood in need of no other certificate than his dialect." Which shows that what our French friend is speaking of was not a Palatine nor a planter, but a genuine Paddy—and no mistake about it. His sincerity was never called in question; he was supposed to have a sympathy with suffering, and every one decided, as it were intuitively, in his favor. "Indeed," he adds, "their conduct in the late war amply justified their favorable opinion, for whilst the Irish emigrant was fighting the battles of America by sea and land, the Irish merchants, principally of Charleston, Baltimore, and Philadelphia, labored with indefatigable zeal at all hazards to promote the spirit of enterprise, and increase the wealth and maintain the credit of the country. Their purses always were opened, and their persons devoted to the country's cause, and on more than one imminent occasion Congress itself, and the very existence of America, probably, owed its preservation to the fidelity and firmness of the Irish. I had the honor," he says, " of dining with an Irish society, composed of the wealthiest merchants and others of the city, in the city tavern of Philadelphia, on St. Patrick's Day." Mr. Froude must not run away with the assertion that the Irish merchants of Charleston and Baltimore and Philadelphia were the Puritan settlers. If they had been, they would have gone home and eaten a cold dinner on St. Patrick's Day.

So much for America and Ireland's relations with her. When the English government asked for four thousand Irish soldiers to go out and fight Americans, they offered to send to Ireland four thousand Protestant Hessians, and the Irish Parliament had the grace to refuse the Hessians. They said "No! If the country is in danger we can arm some of our Protestant people, and they can keep the peace."

Out of this sprang the "Volunteers of '82." Mr. Froude has little or nothing to say of them, consequently, as I am answering, or trying to answer him, I must restrict also their record. Ireland, in 1776, began to arm. This movement was altogether a Protestant one, and confined to the North. The Catholics of Ireland were ground, as it were, into the very dust. No sooner, however, did the Catholics hear that their

Protestant oppressors were **anxious to** do something for the old land, than they came and said to them, "We will forgive everything you have done to us; we will **leave you the** land of Ireland, the wealth and the **commerce; all we ask** of you is to let us help you **for our common** country." At first they were refused, and, **my** friends, when they found they would not be allowed to enter the ranks of the Volunteers, they had the generosity, out of their poverty, **to** collect money and hand it over to clothe the army of their Protestant fellow-citizens. Anything for Ireland. Anything for the man that would lift his hand up for Ireland, no matter what his religion **was**. The old generous spirit was there; **the love** that never could be extinguished was **there**; self-sacrificing as of old; aye, **the** strong love **for any** man, no matter who **he was, that** was a friend of their native land.

But after a time our Protestant friends **in the** Volunteers began to think that these Catholics, after all, were fine, strapping fellows. Somehow, centuries of persecution could not knock the manhood out of them. "They be strong men," says an old writer, "and can bear more of hard living, hunger, and thirst, than any other people that **we know of.**" God knows **their** capabilities of enduring **nakedness,** hunger, **and** thirst, and every other form **of misery,** were **well tested**?

Accordingly, we **find that** in 1780 **there** were fifty thousand Catholics amongst the Volunteers—every man of them with arms in his hands. **Mr.** Froude says that Grattan—the immortal Grattan—that whilst he wished well for Ireland—that whilst he was irreproachable in every way, public or private—that at this time he was guilty of a great mistake. England, says the historian, had long ruled Ireland badly, but had learned a lesson from America, and she was now anxious to govern Ireland well, and no sooner was an abuse pointed out than it was immediately remedied, and if just laws were wanted they were immediately granted; and the mistake Grattan made was that instead of insisting on just legislation from England, he insisted for the legitimate independence of Ireland; that the Irish should have the making of their own laws. Thus, according to Mr. Froude, the energies of the nation, which were wasted in political contention, could have been husbanded to induce England to grant just and fair laws. But he goes on the assumption, my dear American friends and others—the gentleman goes on the assumption that England was willing to redress grievances, to repeal the bad laws and make good ones, and he proves this assertion by saying "that she struck off of the wrists of the Irish merchants the chains of their commercial slavery, and that she restored to Ireland her trade." You remember that this trade was taken away from them: the woollen trade, and nearly every other form of trade was discountenanced or ruined.

Now, I wish for the sake of the honor of England that she was as generous, or even as just, as Mr. Froude represents her, and as he no doubt would wish her to be; but we have the fact before us that in 1779, when a movement was made to repeal the laws restricting the commerce of Ireland, the English Parliament, the English King, the Lord Lieutenant of Ireland, and the English Government opposed it to the very death. They would not have it—not one fetter would they strike off from the chain that encumbered even the Protestants and the planters of Ireland. And it was only when Grattan rose up in the Irish Parliament and insisted that Ireland should get back her trade—it was only then that England consented — because there were fifty thousand armed Volunteers outside.

The state of Ireland at the time is thus described: "Such is the state of the Constitution that three millions of good, faithful subjects in their native land are excluded from every trust, power, and emolument in the state, civil and military; excluded from all corporate rights and immunities; excluded from grand juries, and restrained in petty juries; excluded in every direction from every trust, from every incorporated society, and from every establishment, occasional or fixed, that was instituted for public defense; from the bank, from the bench, from the exchange, from the university, from the college of physicians—from what were they not excluded?" asks the writer. "There is no institution which the wit of man has invented, or the progress of society has produced, which private charity or public munificence has founded for the advancement of education around us, for the permanent relief of age, infirmity, and misfortune, from the participation of the benefits of which, on all occasions, the Catholics of Ireland were not carefully excluded."

Grattan rose up in the Senate, and, lifting up his heroic hand and voice to heaven, he swore before the God of justice that this should come to an end. The English Government heard him with a determination as great as that of the Irish patriot, and swore equally that this should remain the law. Was it not time to assert for Ireland her independence? Mr. Froude claims that England willingly consented to give up the restrictions on Irish commerce when Grattan proposed it in the House. An official of the government, named Hussey Burgh, rose up, to the astonishment of the government, and seconded Grattan's resolution, to the rage and consternation of the government factions, as was shown by the unequivocal demonstration of the executive of the ministerial bench. Hussey Burgh was one of the most fascinating men of the day; he, of whom it was thought patriotism was impossible, moved " That we take up the question, and represent to his Majesty that it was not by any temporary expedients, but by free trade alone, that this nation is now to be saved from impending ruin."

While they were fighting the government within, Grattan took good care to have the Volunteers drawn out in the streets of Dublin—there they were in their thousands—armed men, drilled men—and they had their cannons with them, and about the mouths of the guns they had tied a label, or card, with these words: " Free Trade for Ireland, or else ——."

## Grattan and the Volunteers. 187

So it happened that Lord North was obliged, greatly against his will, to introduce measures to restore to Ireland her trade. Now, I ask, was not Henry Grattan justified, seeing that it was only at the cannon's mouth he could obtain justice from the Parliament of England, when he said: "This English Parliament will never do us justice, and, in the name of God, now that we have our men armed around us, let us demand for Ireland the perfect independence of the people from the Parliament of England, and the right to make whatever laws that are most conducive to the welfare of our own people."

It is perfectly true that Grattan failed; it is perfectly true that although that declaration of independence was proclaimed by law, and, as Mr. Froude observes, " Home Rule was tried in Ireland from '82 to '99, and it was a failure "—all this is true; but why was it so, my friends? Reflect upon this; the Irish Parliament did not represent the nation. The Irish Parliament consisted of three hundred members, and of these three hundred there were only seventy-two that were elected by the people; all the others were " nomination boroughs," as they were called. Certain great lords, barons, and noblemen had three or four little towns on their estates, which towns returned a Member of Parliament; and the poor people who had the votes were at the mercy of the landlord, who made the regular " nominations," and put up whom he desired, and the people were compelled to vote for him or suffer the consequences. Just as, in the Protestant church, whenever a bishop dies, the queen comes and writes to the clergy and says: You will name such a one for bishop—and then they elect him. Even the seventy-two who were in some sense representatives of the people, whom did they represent? There were nearly three millions of Irishmen in Ireland, men of intellect and of education, in spite of all the laws that were made against schools and colleges for Catholics; there were nearly three millions of Irish Catholics in the land, and not a man of them had a vote even for a Member of Parliament. And, therefore, this wretched parliament, that only represented one-tenth of the nation, if it was venal and corrupt, is no disgrace to the Irish people, and is no argument or imputation that they did not know how to govern themselves.

Meantime, the Volunteers made the most tremendous mistake, and that was by letting Catholics in amongst their ranks. Here I have my Lord Sheffield. Here is what he says:—it will give you clearly to understand, ladies and gentlemen of America, how the English people looked upon us Irish one hundred years ago; indeed, according to Cobbett, one of their most distinguished writers, this was how they looked upon you, until you taught them with the sword to look upon you with more respect: "It is now necessary," says Lord Sheffield, "to go back to the year 1778, to take notice of a phenomenon which began to appear at that time; it is a wonderful thing." What was it? "The like has never been seen in any country, at least where there was an established government. To describe it: it is an army unauthorized by the law, and unnatural; and generally known by the name of the Volunteers of Ireland. The arms issued from the public stores were insufficient to supply the rapid increase of the Volunteers; the rest were procured by themselves, and the necessary accoutrements, with a considerable number of field-pieces. The Opposition in England speak highly of them; and the supporters of the government in both countries mention them with civility." (It is not easy to be uncivil to an army of ninety-five thousand men.) "The wonderful efforts of England in America were, somehow or other, wasted to no purpose." The wonderful efforts of England in America were wasted to no purpose! There happened to be a man in the way, and that man was George Washington.

He goes on to speak of the Volunteers. The "many-headed monster," as he calls it, "now began to think it would be proper to reform the State and to purge the Parliament of Ireland." Henry Grattan said, "I will never claim freedom for six hundred thousand of my countrymen while I leave two million or more of them in chains. Give the Catholics of Ireland their civil rights and their franchise; give them the power to return members to the Irish Parliament, and let the nation be represented; put an end to the rotten nomination boroughs; let the members represent the people truly, and you will have reformed your Parliament, and you will have established for ever the liberties which the Volunteers have won."

This was what the Volunteers wanted; and for this they got, from my Lord Sheffield, the very genteel name of "the many-headed monster." But they did something still more strange than this. "So far," he says, "everything went on as might have been expected. But there is another part of their conduct neither natural nor rational. Some of the corps, for the purpose of increasing their numbers, perhaps, or possibly without consideration, admitted Roman Catholics." (They must have been mad. They did it "without consideration.") "And others, perhaps, enrolled them latterly for the sake of acquiring numbers and strength to force a reform of the government from England"—(to force a reform which the government of England would never permit, because she wanted to have a rotten parliament to her hand, and through that parliament to destroy the country.) "Well, but that Protestants should allow and encourage this also, and form a whole corps of Roman Catholics, when all Europe was at peace, is scarcely to be believed—above all, in view of their number. It has become the system of the Roman Catholics to enroll as many as possible, particularly since the peace of last summer; and there is nothing unequivocal in this. Already, perhaps five thousand of these are in arms, and in a year or less they may be ten thousand. All the Protestants are gradually quitting the service; and the only Protestants are those who continue since the peace, in order to prevent the Volunteer arms from falling into more dangerous hands, and to counterbalance the Catholics." Then he goes on to say: "**They are** many. If they were only one-fifth, instead of four-fifths, of the people, the writer of this observation would be the last man to suggest a difficulty about their being admitted into power, or every right or advantage given to them. **But they** do not forget the situation in which their ancestors have been. They are not blind to what they might acquire. Persevering for upwards of two centuries under every discouragement, under every severity, subjected to every disadvantage, does not prove an indifference to the principles of their religion. Thinking as they do, feeling as they do, believing as they do, they would **not be** men if they did not wish for a change. **Nor** would Protestants be worthy of the designation of reasonable creatures if they did not take precautions to prevent it."

Thus, it is to this fact that the English Government steadily opposed reform, that they **would** not hear of reform—because they wanted **to** have a venal, corrupt, miserable seventy-two in their hands,—it is to this fact, and not to any mistake of Grattan, that we owe the collapse of that magnificent revolutionary movement of the "Irish Volunteers."

Well, England now adopted another policy. We have evidence of it. **As soon** as William Pitt came into office as Premier, his first thought **was**—"I will put an end to this Irish difficulty? I will have no more laws made in Ireland, for Irishmen. I will unite the two parliaments into one, and will **not** leave Ireland **a** single shadow **of** legislative independence."

This being the programme, how was it to be worked out? Mr. Froude says, or seems to say, that "the Rebellion of '98 was one of those outbursts of Irish ungovernable passion and of Irish inconstancy, accompanied by cowardice and by treachery, with which" (according to him) "we are all so familiar in the history of Ireland." Now, I have a different account of '98. Mr. Froude says that "the rebellion arose out of the disturbance of men's minds created by the French Revolution;" and, indeed, there is a great deal of truth in this. The French Revolution set all the world in a blaze, and the flame spread, no doubt, to Ireland.

Mr. Froude goes on to say that "the Irish Government were so hampered by this free parliament, this parliament of Grattan's, that although they saw the danger approaching, they could not avert it:—their hands were bound; nay, more," he adds, "the government, bound by constitutional law, and by parliament, could not touch one of the United Irishmen until they had first committed themselves by some overt act of treason; in other words, until they had first risen."

Now, according to this historian, there was nothing done to molest, slay, or persecute the people of Ireland until they rose in arms in '98. My friends, the rising of 1798 took place on the 23d of May. On that day the "United Irishmen" rose. I ask you now to consider whether the government had any share in that rising, or in creating that rebellion?

As early as 1797, the country was beginning to be

disturbed, according to Mr. Froude; and, during the first three months of January, February, and March, in '98, we find Lord Moira giving his testimony as to the action of the English Government. "My Lords," he says, in the House of Lords, "I have seen in Ireland the most absurd, as well as the most disgusting tyranny, that any nation ever groaned under. I have been myself a witness of it in many instances; I have seen it practiced unchecked, and the effects that have resulted from it have been such as I have stated to your lordships. I have seen in that country a marked distinction between the English and the Irish. I have seen troops that have been sent there full of this prejudice—that every inhabitant of that kingdom is a rebel to the British Government." Troops were sent there before the rebellion, and told—" every man you meet is a rebel." "I have seen most wanton insults practiced upon men of all ranks and conditions."

They sent their thousands into Ireland in preparation for the rebellion; they had, between Welsh and Scotch and Hessian regiments, and between English and Irish militia, an army of one hundred and thirty thousand men prepared for the work; and in this way they goaded the people on to rebellion. The rack, indeed, was not at hand, but the punishment of " picketing " was in practice, which had been for some years abolished as too inhuman even for the treatment of savages.

Lord Moira goes on to say that he had known of a man who, in order to extort confession of a crime from him, was "picketed" until he actually fainted ("picketing" meant putting them on the point of a stake upon one foot), "and picketed a second time until he fainted again; and again, as soon as he came to himself, picketed the third time until he fainted once more, and all this on mere suspicion."

Not only was this punishment used, but every species of torture. Men were taken and hung up until they were half dead, and then threatened with a repetition of the cruel torture unless they made confession of imputed guilt. They sent their soldiers into the country, and quartered them at what was called "free quarters." The English yeomanry and the Orange yeomanry of Ireland lived upon the people; they violated the women, they killed the aged, they plundered the houses, they set fire to the villages, they exercised every form of torture the most terrible—this terrible soldiery. All this took place before a single rising in Ireland, before the rebellion of '98 sprung up at all. We had a brave and gallant man sent to Ireland at that time—Sir Ralph Abercrombie; and he declared he was so frightened and disgusted at the conduct of the soldiers that he threw up his commission, and refused to take the command of the forces in Ireland. He issued a general order in February, '98—the rebellion did not begin until May—he began his general order with these words: "The very disgraceful frequency of great cruelties and crimes, and the many complaints of the conduct of the troops in this kingdom, has too unfortunately proved the army to be in a state of licentiousness that **renders it formidable to** every one, except **the enemy." Then he t**hrew up his commission in disgust; and General Lake was sent to command in Ireland. He says: "The state of the country **and its occupation** previous to the insurrection, **is not to be** imagined, **except by** those **who** witnessed the atrocities of **every description** committed **by the military and the** Orangemen, **that** were let **loose upon** the unfortunate **and** defenseless population." **Then** he **gives** a long **list of** terrible hangings, burnings, **and** murderings. We read that "**at** Dunlavin, **in** the county of Wicklow," previous to the **rising, "thirty-four** men were shot without any trial." But it **is useless to** enumerate or continue the list **of cruelties perpetrated.** It will suffice **to** say that **where the military** were placed **on free quarters all kinds of crimes were** committed ; **but the** people were **no worse off than** those living **where no soldiers** were quartered ; **for in the latter places** the inhabitants were called to their **doors and** shot without ceremony, and every house was plundered or burned. Nay, more ! We have Mr. Emmet, in his examination, giving his evidence, and **declaring** that it was the fault of the govern**ment,** this Rebellion of '98. The Lord Chancellor **put the following** question to Mr. Emmet : " **Pray, Mr. Emmet,"**—this was in August, '98—" what caused **the** late **insurrection ?"** to which Mr. **Emmet** replied, " **Free quarters, house-burnings, tortures, and all the military** executions **in the** counties of Kildare, Carlow, **and** Wicklow." Before the insurrection broke **out, numbers of** houses, with their furniture, in which concealed arms had been found, were demolished. Numbers of people were daily scourged, picketed, and otherwise put to death, to force confession of concealed crime or plots. Outrageous acts of severity were often committed, even by persons not in the regular troops. And we have the evidence of the brave Sir John Moore, the hero of Corunna. He was in Ireland at the time, in military command, and he bears this testimony. Speaking of Wicklow, the very hotbed of the insurrection, he says, that "moderate treatment by the generals, and the preventing of the troops from pillaging and molesting the people, would soon restore tranquillity; the latter would certainly be quiet if the yeomanry would behave with tolerable decency, and not seek to gratify their ill-humor and revenge upon the poor."

We have the testimony of Sir William Napier, not an Irishman, but a brave English soldier, saying, "What manner of soldiers were these fellows who were let loose upon the wretched districts in which the Ascendency were placed, killing, burning, and confiscating every man's property; and, to use the venerable Abercrombie's words, 'they were formidable to everybody but the enemy.' We ourselves were young at the time; yet, being connected with the army, we were continually among the soldiers, listening with boyish eagerness to their experiences: and well we remember, with horror, to this day, the tales of lust, of bloodshed, and pillage, and the recital of their foul actions against the miserable peasantry, which they used to relate."

I ask you, in all this goading of the people into rebellion, who was accountable if not the infamous government which, at the time, ruled the destinies of Ireland? I ask you, are the Irish people accountable, if from time to time the myrmidons of England have been let loose upon them, ravaging them like tigers, violating every instinct of Irish love of land, of Irish purity, of Irish faith? Is it not a terrible thing that, after all these provocations, which they deliberately put before the people, in order to goad them into the rebellion of '98, and so prepare the way for that union of 1800 which followed that, Mr. Froude says: "Several hot-headed priests put themselves at the head of their people." There was a Father John Murphy in the county of Wexford. He came home from his duties one day, to find the houses of the poor people around sacked and burned; to find his unfortunate parishioners huddled about the blackened walls of the chapel, crying: "Soggarth dear, what are we to do? where are we to fly from this terrible persecution that has come upon us?" And Father John Murphy got the pikes, put them in their hands, and put himself at their head! So you see, my friends, there are two sides to every story.

My friends, I have endeavored to give you some portions of the Irish side of the story, basing my testimony upon the records of Protestant and English writers, and upon the testimony which I have been so proud to put before you, of noble, generous, American gentlemen. I have to apologize for the dryness of the subject, and the imperfect manner in which I have treated it, and also for the unconscionable length of time in which I have tried your patience. On next Tuesday evening we shall be approaching ticklish ground:—"Ireland since the Union;" Ireland as she is to-day; and Ireland, as my heart and brain tell me she shall be in some future day.

## LECTURE V.

# IRELAND SINCE THE UNION.

———•••———

MR. FROUDE opens his fifth and last lecture by stating that the Irish left the paths of practical reform, and clamored for political agitation. Now, I am quite as much opposed to political agitation as Mr. Froude. I regard it as an evil, distracting men's minds from the more important and necessary duties of life, withdrawing their attention from business, and the sober pursuit of industry, creating animosities and bad blood between citizens, affording an easy and profitable employment to many a worthless demagogue, and frequently (in fact, in most cases) bringing to the surface the worst and meanest elements of society. But we must not forget that political agitation, with all these drawbacks, is the only resource of a people who endeavor to obtain just laws from an unwilling government. What were the struggles of the seventeenth century in France, Germany, and the Low Countries, with which Mr. Froude sympathises so deeply, but political agitation, deepening into the form of armed revolt, in order to extort from the various governments just measures of toleration and liberty of conscience. For these and such as these, Mr. Froude has words of admiration and sympathy, although the people in arms were really innovators, seeking to destroy a state of things established for ages; but for the Irish, merely standing on the defensive against an innovating and revolutionary government, and seeking to preserve, not freedom, for that was already gone, but land, life, conscience, and their ancient creed, this learned gentleman has no words but reproof, condemnation, and disdain. In 1780 the Irish people, mostly the Protestant portion of them, labored for the repeal of certain laws, restricting and annihilating the trade and industry of the people. Was England willing to grant this measure of justice? Was she only anxious, as Mr. Froude says, to remedy every evil as soon as it was pointed out? I answer No, and my proof lies here; that free trade, as it was called, was extorted and forced from the government by the presence of fifty thousand armed Volunteers, who planted their cannon in the streets of Dublin and attached to each gun the significant label " Free Trade or ———" If every measure of just legislation was only to be obtained by such means as these, the country would of necessity be kept in a state of perpetual revolution. What wonder, then, that the Irish thought with Henry Grattan, that it would be better to have their own parliament, free and independent of that of England, to legislate for the wants and interests of their own country. Thus we see that the action of 1782 was the result, not of the love of the Irish people for political agitation, but of Ireland's well-founded conviction that she never could expect or obtain just and salutary legislation except from her own parliament, free and independent. It is true that this independent Irish parliament failed to realize the hopes of the Irish nation, and Mr. Froude accounts for it by saying that the Irish are incapable of home legislation. I say that the cause of this failure lay in the fact that the parliament of eighty-two did not represent the nation at all. Nearly three millions of Irishmen, the vast majority of the people, were unrepresented. They had not even a vote for a single member of that parliament, which represented about half a million of Protestant strangers, English and Scotch, who had recently settled in Ireland. But even these men were not fairly represented, as the constitution of the parliament will prove. The House of Commons was made up of three hundred members. Of these only seventy-two were elected by the people. The rest represented rotten or nomination boroughs, and were the mere nominees, and consequently the agents, of certain great lords and extensive landed proprietors. Had the nation been represented they would have solved the problem of home rule in favor of Ireland, despite the corruption which must always be found in large assemblies. The Irish people knew this, and loudly proclaimed that the parliament should be reformed on the basis of a truly national representation;

the volunteers cried out for reform, and at their first meeting at Dungannon they decided, to their honor, that every Irishman had a right to be represented. The United Irishmen, who in the beginning were not a secret society, laid down as their fundamental principles the three following resolutions : 1st, That the weight of English influence in the government of this country is so great as to require a cordial union among all the people of Ireland, to maintain that balance which is essential to the preservation of our liberties, and the extension of our commerce. 2d, That the sole constitutional mode by which this influence can be opposed, is by a complete and radical reform of the representation of the people in parliament. 3d, That no reform is just which does not include every Irishman of every religious persuasion. Who opposed and hindered the reform which would have made the Irish parliament a truly representative body instead of the hideous sham of a corrupt party clique, as it was? I answer, the government of England. On the 29th of November, 1783, Mr. Flood introduced into the Irish Parliament a bill of reform. Who led the opposition to it? Mr. Yelverton, the Attorney-General of the government, gave the idea of a reform of parliament *an official opposition*. The vote was secured by corrupting the venal members, and the bill was thrown out by a division of one hundred and fifty to seventy-seven. The Attorney-General then moved "That it had now become necessary to declare that the House would maintain its just rights and privileges against all encroachments whatsoever." Their just rights and privileges being to represent a faction, and to exclude from all representation five-sixths of the people of Ireland. " From agitation grew conspiracy," says Mr. Froude, "and from conspiracy rebellion." In these words the historian alludes to the Society of United Irishmen, out of which grew the Rebellion of '98. I have shown, on the evidence of such men as Sir Ralph Abercrombie and Sir John Moore, that the rebellion of '98 was mainly the work of the English Government. We have also seen that the United Irishmen were, in the beginning, far from being a secret society or conspiracy. But the principle on which they were founded, was " Union amongst all Irishmen," and this was enough to alarm the government, whose policy it has ever been to rule Ireland through the divisions amongst her people. England's Premier, therefore, Wm. Pitt, resolved to disarm the Volunteers (who were doomed from the moment they fraternized with the Catholics, and admitted them into their ranks), to force the United Irishmen to become a secret conspiracy, and to bring on, through them, a rebellion in Ireland. The first of these designs he accomplished by raising the standing army to fifteen thousand men, in 1785, and by obtaining a grant of £20,000 to clothe and organize the militia. The second was achieved in 1793, by the passing of the gunpowder and convention bills. A public meeting of United Irishmen was held in Dublin in February, 1793, to protest against the inquisitorial and tyrannical nature of certain proceedings of the secret committee of the

House of Lords. For this the Honorable Mr. Butler, who presided at the meeting, and Mr. Oliver Bond, who acted as secretary, were imprisoned for six months and fined £500 each. The Society of United Irishmen, thus persecuted, took refuge in secrecy and became a conspiracy. It was still, however, watched and fomented by government. The first really treasonable project was proposed to it in April, 1794, by the Rev. Wm. Jackson, a Protestant clergyman and an agent from the French Convention, and he was accompanied by a London lawyer named John Cockayne, an agent of Wm. Pitt, the Premier of England. Thus did the Society of United Irishmen become a secret and treasonable conspiracy. Their first organization was perfectly open, legitimate, and loyal, but their object was union amongst Irishmen, and this did not answer the purposes of the English Government, so they must be got rid of. The only way to do this was to goad them into conspiracy by persecution, and from conspiracy to rebellion, which could be suppressed, and so lay the country once more prostrate at the feet of the minister. The test of the United Irishmen reveals nothing treasonable. It was as follows: "I, A. B., in the presence of God, do pledge myself to my country, that I will use all my abilities and influence in the attainment of an impartial and adequate representation of the Irish nation in parliament; and as a means of absolute and immediate necessity in the establishment of this chief good of Ireland, I will endeavor, as much as lies in my ability, to forward a brotherhood of affection and identity of interests, a communion of rights, and an union of power among Irishmen of all religious persuasions, without which every reform in parliament must be partial, not national, inadequate to the wants, delusive to the wishes, and insufficient for the freedom and happiness of this country." That Wolfe Tone was imbued with republican and revolutionary ideas I do not deny, but he never attempted to impress these on the society, nor did they ever find way into its councils, until the English Government forced it to become a conspiracy. The third object of the Premier and the government, namely, to create an Irish rebellion, was accomplished by the cruelty and abominations of the soldiery quartered on the people—cruelties which made death itself preferable to life, as we have seen in the last lecture. So much for Mr. Froude's assertions that "The Irish left the paths of practical reform, and clamored for political agitation. From agitation grew conspiracy, and from conspiracy rebellion."

It may be asked what motive could the English Premier have in adopting so tortuous a policy. I answer, he had resolved on the legislative Union of England and Ireland by the destruction of the Irish Parliament, and he knew that it was through the humiliation and misfortune, not through the happiness and prosperity of Ireland, that such a measure could be brought about. "To realize his favorite project," says an Irish historian, "the unhappy country was to be deluged with crime and blood." And yet how easy it was to govern Ireland, and to conciliate the affections of her people, Pitt himself had a striking proof of at this very time. In 1795, the Premier seemed to abandon for a time his theory of governing Ireland by coercion and terror. The Earl of Westmoreland was recalled from Ireland and Earl Fitzwilliam arrived to replace him, on the 4th of January, 1795.

Lord Fitzwilliam was a man of liberal principles and most estimable disposition. He came to Ireland on the express understanding that he was to be at liberty to pursue a policy of conciliation and kindness. He found at Dublin Castle, Secretary Cook and the Beresfords, who had monopolized for years all the public offices and emoluments, and had uncontrolled sway over the Irish Government. He dismissed them all and surrounded himself with liberal-minded men. The Catholics were promised emancipation, the people, were inspired with a confidence which they never felt before, universal joy spread through the nation, and every idea of disaffection or rebellion seemed at once to vanish from the public mind. In an evil hour Pitt resumed his old ideas, and on the 25th of March, after a term of little more than two months, Earl Fitzwilliam was recalled. The effect was heartrending. Addresses and resolutions poured in from all sides to avert the calamity, but to no purpose. Fitzwilliam left amidst the anguish of the people, who were exasperated at Pitt's duplicity. The earl's coach was drawn to the waterside by some of the leading citizens of Dublin, and the city, as well as the nation, wore an aspect of mourning. The fact was, Pitt had made up his mind to carry the union. The rebellion broke out and was defeated, and truly, as Mr. Froude remarks, "the victors took away old privileges and made the yoke heavier." The "old privilege" in question was the Irish Parliament. I believe that America, to which Mr. Froude makes appeal, looks upon home legislation as *the right*, not the privilege, of a people. Looking back to strengthen his argument, the learned gentleman stated that the penal laws of Elizabeth were the effect and result of the revolutionary war of 1600, by which I presume he means the war of Hugh O'Neill, in Ulster. Now, history records that the penal laws began to operate in Ireland as early as 1534, under Henry VIII. In 1537, Cromer, the Primate, was cast into prison for denying the royal supremacy. Passing over the succeeding penalties enacted by Henry and by Edward VI., we come to the parliament convoked by Elizabeth in 1560. In that famous assembly, "All officers and ministers, ecclesiastic or lay, were bound to take the oath of supremacy under pain of forfeiture and total incapacity; and any one who maintained the spiritual supremacy of the Pope was to forfeit, for the first offence, all his estates, real and personal, or to be imprisoned for one year, if not worth £20; for the second offence to be liable to præmunire, and for the third to be guilty of high treason." These laws were made, and commissioners were appointed to enforce them, full forty years before the revolution to which Mr. Froude alludes as the revolution of 1600. How then can that gentleman ask us to regard the penal laws as the effects of that revolution? Moreover, does he not himself tell us that Elizabeth was forced into the enactment of penal laws by the political necessities of her situation? He excuses her cruelties by pleading that she could not help herself. If Ireland was permitted to remain Catholic, Ireland would be hostile to her, and the natural and necessary ally of her enemies, therefore Ireland's Catholicity was to be destroyed in order to preserve the integrity of her empire. The only way to effect this was by penal laws making it felony to be a Catholic in Ireland; and so Elizabeth, on the principle of self-preservation, was constrained to make these laws. This is Mr. Froude's own argument, put forth in his second lecture; yet, in his fifth and last lecture he turns round and tells us that these penal laws were the consequence of a revolution which took place nearly forty years after they were enacted. I would advise the learned gentleman, seeing the manner in which he treats history, to sacrifice to Mercury for the gift of a better memory.

"The laws against Catholics were almost repealed before 1798." This is the next assertion of Mr. Froude. Now, I beg my reader to consider what these large measures of indulgence were. In 1771, parliament passed an act to enable a Catholic to take a long lease of fifty acres of bog, to which, if the bog were too deep for a foundation, half an acre of arable land might be added for a house; but this holding should not be within a mile of any city or town; and if half the bog were not reclaimed within twenty-one years, the lease was forfeited. Beggarly as this concession was, it was found necessary in order to conciliate the furious Protestant faction, to counterbalance it by an act adding £10 a year to the pension of £30 offered to any "Popish priest duly converted to the Protestant religion." In October, 1777, the news reached England that Gen. Burgoyne had surrendered to the American Gen. Gates, and Lord North immediately expressed an ardent desire to relax the penal laws. In January, 1778, the independence of the United States was acknowledged by France, and immediately the English Parliament passed a bill for the relief of the Roman Catholics. In the May of the same year, the Irish Parliament passed a bill enabling the Catholics to lease land for 999 years, repealing the unnatural law which altered the succession in favor of a child embracing Protestantism, and also the law for the prosecution of priests and for the imprisonment of Catholic schoolmasters. This, together with the act of 1793, restoring the franchise to Catholics, and enabling them to hold certain commissions in the army, was positively all that was granted, and this Mr. Froude has the hardihood to call an almost total repeal of the acts against Catholics.

"The insurrection of '98," continues the learned gentleman, "threw Ireland back into a condition of confusion and misery from which she was partially delivered by the act of union." The first part of this proposition I admit, the second I emphatically deny.

I freely admit that Ireland was flung into a state of confusion and misery by the movement of '98. An unsuccessful rebellion is one of the greatest calamities that can befall a people, and the sooner Irish patriots understand this the better will it be for them and for their country. But I must deny that the act of union was even a partial deliverance from that misery, or a benefit or blessing of any kind for Ireland. It was a curse, and nothing more nor less; an evil which must be remedied if the wrongs and miseries of Ireland are ever to be redressed. I need not dwell on the wholesale corruption and other execrable means by which the political apostate Castlereagh carried the vile measure. Mr. Froude has the good sense not to meddle with the dirty subject, and I can do no better than to imitate him in this. "It was expected," he says, "that whatsoever grievances Ireland complained of would be removed by legislation." Quite true. The nation was bribed by promises of justice, as the politicians were bribed by money and titles. Amongst other things, Catholic Emancipation was promised as a bribe for the surrender of the native parliament. But when the wicked act was consummated, the Irish were left to

"Mourn the hopes that left them,"

and to meditate in bitterness of spirit on the nature of English faith. "But," adds Mr. Froude, "they had no foundation for their complaints. They were not treated unjustly." Good God. What is this gentleman's idea of justice? What did Ireland gain, what did she lose, by the act of union? Her gain is nothing—absolutely **nothing.** Let us examine her loss. The national debt of Ireland was distinct from that of England up to the year 1817. In 1797, just before the insurrection, the national debt of Ireland was less than four millions sterling. Three years later that debt was found to be £26,841,219. If you ask me the reason of the enormous increase, I answer: first, England had for her own purposes in Ireland at the time of the union 126,500 men. She made Ireland pay for every man of them. In order to carry the union, England spent enormous sums in bribes to spies, informers, and Members of Parliament. She **took every** penny of this money out of the **Irish treasury.** There were eighty-four rotten **boroughs** disfranchised, **and** to compensate those who lost the nomination to these boroughs, that is to say, who lost the **bribery** money and corrupt influence which the representation of these boroughs brought them, Castlereagh gave a sum of £1,200,000. Ireland was made to pay this **money** by which England purchased the union. "It was strange," says O'Connell, "that Ireland was not made to pay for the knife with which, twenty-two **years** later, Castlereagh cut his throat." But if Ireland's **debt** was run up from less than four millions **to nearly** twenty-seven millions in so short a time, mark what follows. In January, 1801, the debt of **Great** Britain was £450,504,984, the annual charge for which was £17,718,851. In 1817, the same debt was £734,522,104, the **annual** charge being £28,238,416. Thus we see that the debt of England **was** not quite doubled during these years of most expensive war. Now, come to Ireland for the same time. In 1801, the Irish debt was £28,545,134, at an annual charge of £1,244,463. In 1817, the same Irish debt was £112,704,773, at an annual charge of £4,104,514. Now reflect upon these figures. Ireland was so lightly burthened with debt at the time of the union, as compared with England, that the English did not presume to ask us to bear an equal taxation with themselves. They were rich and could bear it. We were poor and could not. Before the union England had an enormous debt of £450,000,000. Ireland, a comparatively trifling debt of £26,000,000. Ireland was consequently much more lightly taxed than England, as it is much easier to pay interest on £26 than on £450. It was, however, agreed that in case the debt of Ireland ever arrived at one-seventh of that of England, then Ireland should be subject to indiscriminate taxation with Great Britain. An English Chancellor of the Exchequer took charge of Ireland's accounts, for the keeping our own books was lost to us by the union: "The debt of England went on increasing rapidly," says Mr. Mitchel, "owing to the war and subsidies to all enemies of France, the debt of Ireland was somehow found to increase more than twice as fast as that of England—as if Ireland had a *double* interest in crushing France." In a word, while the Imperial Parliament at Westminster less than doubled the debt of England, they managed to increase Ireland's debt four-fold in sixteen years, and so made the Irish people liable to be taxed for the enormous debt which

England had contracted even before the union. And yet Mr. Froude audaciously says, " the people were not treated unjustly." Mr. Froude lays stress on the benefit which the union conferred on Ireland by giving her the same commercial privileges enjoyed by England. " True, the laws regulating trade are the same in the two islands," says Mr. Mitchel. " Ireland *may* export even woollen cloth to England; she *may* import, in her own ships, tea from China, and sugar from Barbadoes; the laws which made those acts penal offences no longer exist; they are no longer needed; England is fully in possession; and by the operation of those old laws, Ireland was utterly ruined. England has the commercial marine; Ireland has it to create. England has the manufacturing skill and machinery, of which Ireland was deprived by express laws for that purpose. England has the current of trade established, setting strongly in her own channel; while Ireland is left dry." "To create, or recover at this day, these great industrial and commercial resources, and that in the face of wealthy rivals already in full possession, is manifestly impossible, without one or other of these two conditions, either immense command of capital, or effectual protective duties. But by the union our capital is drained away to England; and by the union we are deprived of the power of imposing protective duties. It was to this very end that the union was forced upon Ireland, through 'intolerance of Irish prosperity.'" "Do not unite with us, sir," said Dr. Johnson; "*we shall rob you*." In the first year after the union, in 1801, Mr. Foster stated in parliament a falling off in exported linens of five million yards. The same gentleman, three years later, stated that, in 1800, the net produce of the Irish revenue was £2,800,000, whilst the debt was only £25,000,000; whereas, three years later, the debt was £53,000,000, more than doubled, whilst the revenue was £2,789,000, a falling off of £11,000 in the income, to meet a debt more than doubled.

Absenteeism was vastly increased by the union. Dublin was no longer a metropolis. Fashion, wealth, political interest, intellectual activity, all were transferred to London. At this day, the Duke of Leinster's palace is changed into a museum; Powerscourt House is a warehouse for drapers; Tyrone House is a schoolhouse; Bective House has given place to a Presbyterian meeting-house; Charlemont House is the head office of the Board of Works; Aldborough House a barrack: Belvidere House a convent. This, and far worse than this, was the state to which the union brought Ireland. The crumbling liberties of Dublin attest the ruin of her trade; the forsaken harbors of Limerick and Galway tell the destruction of her commerce; the palaces in Dublin abandoned to decay, announce that she has no longer a resident nobility; and the forlorn custom-houses tell that her income is transferred elsewhere. The Catholics were told that their emancipation would be one of the results of the union, and, upon this understanding, plainly enough given by my Lord Cornwallis, some of the bishops gave a tacit and neutral kind of consent to the measure. The word of the government was pledged. Pitt's honor was at stake. He had pledged himself through his Lord Lieutenant Cornwallis "not to embark in the service of government, except on the terms of the Catholic privileges being obtained." Pitt retired on pretence that the king's obstinacy prevented him from keeping his word.

But it is well known that the reason why Pitt retired was, that his continental policy had failed; that the people of England were tired of his wars, and that they were clamoring for peace. He was too proud a man to sign even a temporary peace with France, and so he retired in sullen pride and disgust, and he put his retirement on the easy pretence that he could not be allowed to carry out Catholic emancipation. Some time after the Addington administration was broken up, Mr. Pitt returned again to the Premiership of England; and the second time not one word escaped his lips about Catholic Emancipation, a thing he resisted to the day of his death. He was as great an enemy of the Catholics of Ireland, as ever poor old, foolish, mad George III. was, and it was only after twenty-nine years of marked effort that the great O'Connell rallied the Irish nation; that he succeeded after a time in uniting all the Catholics of Ireland as one man, and a great number of her noble-hearted Protestant fellow-Irishmen. When O'Connell came knocking at the doors of the British Parliament with the hands of the united Irish people; when he spoke with the voice of eight millions, only then, even as the walls of Jericho crumbled to the sound of Joshua's trumpet, did the old, bigoted British House of Commons tremble, and did the doors open to the gigantic Irishman that represented them.

The English historian cannot say that England granted Catholic Emancipation willingly. She granted it as a man would yield up a bad tooth to a dentist. O'Connell put the forceps into that false old mouth. The old tyrant wriggled and groaned. The bigoted profligate who then disgraced the English crown shed his crocodile tears upon the bill; the eyes which were never known to weep over the ruin of female virtue; the face that was never known to change color in the presence of any foul deed or accusation of vice—that face grew pale, and George IV. wept for sorrow when he had to sign the Catholic Emancipation Bill. The man who had conquered Napoleon upon the field of Waterloo—the man who was declared to be the invincible victor of the greatest of warriors—stood there with that bill in his hand, and he said to the King of England, "I would not grant, your Majesty, any more than you; but it is forced upon you and me. You must sign that paper or prepare for civil war and rebellion in Ireland."

I regret to be obliged to say it, my friends, but really, the history of my native land proves to me that England never granted anything to Ireland from a sense of justice, or from any other motive than the craven fear of civil war or some serious inconvenience to herself.

Now, having arrived at this point, Mr. Froude glances, I must say, in a magnificent, manly manner over the great questions that have affected Ireland since the day that emancipation was passed.  He speaks words of the most eloquent compassion over the terrible visitation of 1846 and 1847—words, the reading of which brought tears to my eyes—and for those words of compassion he gave to the people whose sufferings I witnessed, I pray to God to bless him and reward him.  He speaks words of generous and enlightened statesmanship and sympathy with the tenant farmers and peasants of Ireland, and for those words, Mr. Froude, if you were an Englishman ten thousand times over, I love you.

He does not attempt to speak of the future of Ireland.  Perhaps it is a dangerous thing for me.  Yet, I suppose all that we have been discussing in the past must have some reference to the future, for surely the verdict that Mr. Froude looks for is not the mere verdict of absolution for past iniquities.  He has come here, though not a Catholic, like a man going to confession.  He has cried out loudly and generously, "We have sinned! we have sinned! we have grievously sinned!"  The verdict which he calls for must surely regard the future more than the past, for how, in the name of common sense, how, in the name of justice and history, can any man ask for a verdict justifying the roll of iniquities, the heart-rending record of cruelty, injustice, bloodshed, and ruin, which we have been contemplating in common with Mr.

Froude. It must be for the future. What is that future to be?

Well, my friends, and first of all, my American grand jury, you must remember that I am only a monk, I am not a man of the world, and I do not understand much about these things. There are wiser men than myself, and I will give you their opinions.

There is one class of men who love Ireland (and I am only speaking the opinion of men who love Ireland, and who love her sincerely), there is one class of men who in their love for Ireland think that the future of their country is to be wrought out by insurrection, by rising in arms against the power which holds Ireland enslaved, if you will. Well, if the history which Mr. Froude has just been telling, and which I have just endeavored to review, teaches anything, it teaches us that there is no use to appeal to the sword or to armed insurrection for Ireland. Mr. Froude says that that will only succeed when the Irish people have two things that they do not seem to have now, namely, union as one man, and a determination not to sheathe that sword until the work is done. I know that I would win louder plaudits from the citizens of America, and speak more popular language in the ears of my fellow-countrymen if I declared my adhesion to that class of Irishmen. But there is not a living man who loves Ireland any more dearly than I do. There are those who love her more effectively and serve her with greater distinction. But there is no living man who loves Ireland more tenderly than I. I prize the good-will of my fellow-Irishmen, and prize it next to the grace of God. I always prized the popularity which, however unworthily, I possessed with them. But I tell you, American citizens, that for all that popularity, and for all that goodwill, I would not compromise one iota of my convictions, nor would I state what I do not believe to be true. I do not believe in insurrectionary movements in so divided a country as Ireland.

There is another class of Irishmen who hold that Ireland has a future and a glorious future, that that future is to be wrought out in this way: they say, and I think with justice and right, that wealth acquired by industry brings with it power and political influence. They say, therefore, to the Irish at home, "Try to accumulate wealth; lay hold of the industries and develope the resources of your country; try, in the meantime, to labor and effect that blessed union, without which, there can never be a future for Ireland. That union can only be effected by largeness of mind, by generosity, by urbanity among fellow-citizens, and by rising above the miserable bigotry that carries religious differences and religious hatred into the relations of life that do not belong to religion." They say to the men of Ireland, "Try to acquire property and wealth; this can only be done by peaceful, arduous industry, and that industry can only be exercised as long as the country is at peace, as long as there is a truce to violent political agitation." Then these men say—I am giving the opinions of others, not my own —to the Irish in America. "Men of Ireland in America—men of Irish birth—men of American birth, but Irish blood—we believe that God has largely entrusted the destinies of Ireland to you. America demands of her citizens only energy, industry, temperance, truth, and obedience to law, and any man that has these, with the brains that God gives to every Irishman, is sure in this country to realize fortune and grand position. If you are faithful to America in these respects, America will be faithful to you. In proportion as the great Irish element in America rise in wealth, it will rise in political influence and power—a political influence and power which, in a few years, is destined to overshadow the whole world, and bring about, through peace and justice, far greater revolution in the cause of honor and in the cause of manhood, than ever have been effected by the sword."

This is the programme of the second class of Irishmen; and now, I tell you candidly, that to this programme I give my heart's and soul's consent.

You will ask me about separation from the crown of England. Well, that is a ticklish question just now. I dare say you remember that when Charles Edward was Pretender to the crown of England, during the first years of the House of Hanover, there was a toast which the Jacobite gentlemen used to give. It was this:

"God bless the King; our noble faith's defender;
Long may he live, and down with the Pretender.
But who be the Pretender, who be King,
God bless us all, that's quite another thing."

And yet, with the courage of an old monk, I will

give you my mind on this very question. History tells us that empires, like men, run the cycle of the years of their life, and then die. No matter how extended their power; no matter how mighty their influence; no matter how great their wealth, or invincible their arms, the day comes—the inevitable day—that brings with it decay and disruption. Thus it was with the empire of the Medes and Persians. Thus it was with the mighty empire of the Assyrians. Thus it was with the Egyptians of old. Thus it was with Greece, and thus with Rome. Who would have imagined, for instance, fifteen hundred years ago, before the Goths first came to the walls of Rome, that the greatest power that was to sway the whole Roman Empire, would be the little unknown island floating out in the Western Ocean, known only by having been conquered by the legions of Rome, and known as the *ultima thule* —the tin island in the far-distant ocean! Yet, in the course of time, this did come to pass.

Now, my friends, England has been a long time at the top of the wheel. Do you imagine she will always remain there? I do not want to be more loyal than Mr. Macaulay, and Mr. Macaulay describes a day which he foresees, when the traveller from New Zealand will take his stand on the broken arch of London Bridge and sketch the ruins of St. Paul's. Is that wheel of England rising or is it falling? Is England to-day what she was twenty years ago? England, twenty years ago, in her first alliance with Napoleon III., had a finger in every pie in Europe. Lord John

Russell and Lord Palmerston were both busy-bodies of the first water. England to-day has no more to say in the affairs of Europe than the Emperor of China. You see it in the fact—I am only talking philosophy—that a few months ago the three great Emperors of Germany, Austria, and Russia came together in Berlin to fix the map of Europe. They didn't even pass England the courtesy to come in and to see what she had to say about it. The army of England is, to-day, nothing; it is a mere cipher. The German emperor can bring 1,200,000 soldiers into the field. England, for the life of her, could not put 200,000 men against him. An English citizen—a loyal Englishman—wrote a book called "The Battle of Dorking," in which he describes the landing of a German army in England, and a battle fought at Dorking, and England without the means of preventing the march of the victorious army upon London. Why should I be more loyal to the English government? Mr. Reed, the first authority in England, and the chief constructor of the Navy, wrote an article the other day, which was published in a London paper, in which he declares that, at this moment, the British fleet would be afraid to go into Russian waters. Why should I be more loyal than Mr. Reed? An empire begins to totter and decay when it withdraws its forces from the outlying provinces, as the decay of the Roman Empire began when the Roman legions were withdrawn from Britain. England to-day says to Canada and Australia, "Oh, take your government into your own hands. I do not want to be bothered with you any more." England, that eighty years ago fought the United Colonies of America as long as she could put a man in the field, has changed her policy. An empire is crumbling to decay when she begins to buy off her enemies, as in the case of the Roman Empire, when she began to buy off the Scythians and Thracians, and the barbarians that came upon her before she fell. A few days ago, England was presented with a little bill by America. She said, "Jonathan, I owe you nothing." John Bull buttoned up his pocket and swore he would not pay a cent. Then America said, "Look here, John, if you don't like this," and he hauled out a sword and put it in one hand, and said, "take whichever you like." John Bull paid the bill. My friends, that looks very much as if the day of the visit of Macaulay's New Zealander was rapidly approaching.

In that day, my position is that Ireland will be the mistress of her own destinies, with the liberty that will come to her, not from men, but from that God whom she ever loved. The whole question is, will Ireland on that day be worthy of the glorious destiny that is in the womb of time and the hand of God? I say that Ireland will be worthy of it, if that day dawn upon a united people, upon a faithful people, upon a people that will keep, every man, his faith in God, his holy religion, as his fathers before him kept it in dark hours and the terrible day of persecution. I say that Ireland will be worthy of the destiny if, on that day, when it dawns upon her, she will be found as distinctive, as individual a people and a race as she is to-day, in her affliction and in her misery. If she foster her traditions, if she keep up her high hopes, if she keep the tender and strong love that her people have always had for the Green Isle that bore them, then will Ireland be worthy in that day of her destiny.

What shall that destiny be? My friends, if Mr. Froude has proved anything, I think he has proved this general proposition, that although the Almighty God lavished upon the English people many gifts, yet there is one gift He never gave them, that of knowing how to govern another people. To govern a people requires, first of all, strict justice; second, to have the interest of the people at heart—their real interests; and, third, it requires tact and urbanity. The French have this, the English have not. Look at Alsace and Lorraine, severed now from the French people, their inhabitants heartbroken, leaving their native land rather than become a part of the German Empire, and why? because France governed her with justice, and always consulted her true interests by French urbanity and tact. The history of the English connection with Ireland is a history of injustice—a history of heartlessness. It is, above all, a history of blundering and want of tact, and not knowing what to do with the people—never understanding them, nor knowing anything about their genius, about their prejudices, or about the shape and form of their national character.

But there is another nation that understands Ireland, and has proved that she understands her; whose statesmen have always spoken words of bright encouragement and tender sympathy, and of manly hope to Ireland, in her darkest days, and that nation is the United States of America. That mighty land, placed by Omnipotent hand between the far east on the one side, to which she stretches out her glorious arm over the broad Pacific, while on the other hand she sweeps with her left hand over the Atlantic and touches Europe—the mighty land, enclosing in her splendid bosom untold resources of every form of commercial and other wealth—the mighty land, with room for three hundred millions of men; with millions of oppressed ones from all the world, ever flying to her more than imperial bosom, there to find liberty, and the sacred right of civil and religious freedom. Is there not reason to suppose that in that future, which we cannot see to-day, but which lies before us, that America will be to the whole world what Rome was in the ancient days, what England was a few years ago — the great store-house of the world, the great ruler—pacific ruler by justice of the whole world; her manufacturing power dispensing from out her mighty bosom all the necessaries and all the luxuries of life to the whole world around her? She may be destined, and I believe she is, to rise rapidly into that gigantic power that will overshadow all other nations. When that conclusion does come to pass, what is more natural than that Ireland—now, I will suppose, mistress of her destinies—should turn and stretch all the arms of her sympathy and love across the intervening waves of the Atlantic, and be received, an independent State, into the mighty confederation of America? Mind--I am not speaking treason. Remember, I said distinctly that all this is to come to pass after Macaulay's New Zealander has arrived. America will require an emporium for her European trade. Ireland lies there, right between her and Europe, with its splendid coast and vast harbors, able to shelter her commercial and other fleets. America may require a great European store-house, and a great European hive for American manufactures. Ireland has manufacturing water-power flowing down to the sea, which in future may be busy in turning wheels set upon those streams by American capital and Irish industry. If ever that day comes; if ever that Union comes, it will be no degradation to Ireland to join hands with America, because America does not enslave her friends. She accepts them on terms of glorious equality, and she respects the rights of the peoples who cast their lots with hers.

Now, I have done with this subject, and with Mr. Froude. I have but one word to say before I retire. If, during the course of these five lectures, one single word personally offensive to this distinguished gentleman has escaped my lips, I take that word back now. I apologize to him before he asks me. I beg to assure him that such a word never came wilfully from my mind or from my heart. He says he loves Ireland. I believe, according to his lights, he does love Ireland. Our lights are very different from his. But still, Almighty God will judge every man according to his lights.

## THE VERDICT.

After the applause had subsided, the Very Rev. Father Starrs, Vicar-General, came forward and said :—

LADIES AND GENTLEMEN: I have merely a few words to say to you before you separate this evening. You all know that this is the last lecture of the course by the Very Rev. Father Burke in reply to the lectures of Mr. Froude, the English historian; and I know very well that you must all feel satisfied with the manner in which he has replied to the lectures of that distinguished gentleman. But nevertheless, I take this opportunity to move a vote of thanks to the Very Rev. Father Burke for the able, dignified, and learned manner in which he has accomplished his purpose, in the course of lectures which he has just concluded.

*Voices.*—I second the motion.

*Father Starrs.*—The motion has been seconded. Are you ready for the question?

*Voices.*—Question! Question!

*Father Starrs.*—All in favor of this motion will please say "Aye."

A tremendous "Aye" resounded in the vast auditorium from pit to dome.

*Father Starrs.*—All opposed will say " No."
No response was heard.
*Father Starrs.*—It is carried unanimously.
[Tremendous applause.]

# APPENDIX.

(1) Page 10. Mr. Froude in his "Reply to Father Burke and Others," denies that he sought such a verdict of acquittal or approbation of England and her policy, from the American people. He states that he only asks the approving force of American opinion, to back him in his opposition to the idea of a repeal of the Union or "Home Rule" as it is called to-day. His leading thought throughout his lectures is, that the Irish don't know how to govern or legislate for themselves; that for them home legislation and an Irish Parliament would be a curse and not a blessing. In order to prove his case, he found it necessary to enter into the history of Ireland, and whilst the question of Irish capability for self-government remains a profound mystery, yet unsolved by experience, Mr. Froude has made it tolerably clear to the American mind that English government in Ireland has been a woeful and disastrous failure. Whether we Irish know how to govern ourselves remains to be seen, but, thanks to Mr. Froude, it is clear that England does not know how to govern us.

(2) Mr. Froude takes me to task for asserting that the Irish by descent in this land are 14,000,000 (I take

no notice of his total of 22,000,000), and he quotes the census of 1870. The reader will perceive that I do not give these figures as my own, but only as the surmises of others, and as what I heard people say. On further inquiry I find that I am not so far from the truth in asserting that the total of Irish birth and descent in this land falls little short of 14,000,000.

(3) Mr. Froude objects to my speculations on the decay of England, inasmuch as I am a British subject in whom he says, "it is scarcely becoming." I cannot see it in this light, and I confess there are few questions on which I speculate with greater pleasure.

(4) Mr. Froude claims to be a grand exception to this rule. He has no contempt, but an exceptional respect for the Irish, of whom he recognizes only two classes, the peasants and the demagogues. The fact of my not being a digger of the soil may explain Mr. Froude's manner of dealing with me, which by the way is a curious illustration of his " exceptional respect for the Irish." How hard a thing it is to be insolent to others (no matter how humble), without lowering onesself! I could scarcely realize the learned historian, the man of name, the elegant, refined graduate of Oxford, when I read of Mr. Froude describing Father Burke as "the raal thing as we say over there," or describing an Irish chieftain of great distinction as "the broth of a boy."

(5) "I do not hate the Catholic religion," says Mr. Froude. I thought he did, and I honored him for it. If the Catholic religion were what Mr. Froude believes it and describes it to be, I should hate and detest it, and so should every honest man. Here is Mr. Froude's

idea and description of the Catholic religion ("Essay on the Condition and Prospects of Protestantism," page 134): "To sacrifice our corrupt inclinations is disagreeable and difficult. To sacrifice bulls and goats in one age, to mutter pater nosters and go to a priest for absolution in another is simple and easy. Priests themselves encourage a tendency which gives them consequence and authority. They need not be conscious rogues, but their convictions go along with their interests, and they believe easily what they desire that others should believe. So the process goes on, the moral element growing weaker and weaker, and at last dying out altogether. Men lose a horror for sin when a private arrangement with a confessor will clear it away. Religion becomes a contrivance to enable them to live for pleasure and to lose nothing by it; a hocus pocus which God is supposed to have contrived to cheat the Devil—a conglomerate of half truths buried in lies." This is Mr. Froude's idea of the Catholic religion, and yet he tells us he does not hate it. Great God!

(6) Although Mr. Froude disclaims this and says that he asks for no such verdict, yet I must remind the reader, that he held up for the admiration of the American people such men as Henry VIII. and Oliver Cromwell. Now it is not these men but their principles and policy which Mr. Froude canonizes, and whoever endorses him is an avowed admirer and abettor of religious persecution the most atrocious.

(7) Mr. Froude says that "order was growing out of the fighting" everywhere but in Ireland. Whoever reads the history of Ireland fairly will perceive that, out

of all the turmoil and confusion of the time, order was rapidly growing and a return to first sanctity, at the time when the Norman invasion came to check that growth and to throw Ireland back into greater confusion and misery than that from which she had escaped.

(8) Mr. Froude takes strong exception to my assertion that England was demoralized at this time, and appeals to her intellectual and physical prestige and power. I am speaking of spiritual demoralization, and the strange spirit of indifference which seemed to possess so many, and which alone can account for the action of a Parliament and a people prepared to accept every mad whim of Henry and Elizabeth as religion.

(9) Mr. Froude attaches little importance to the letter of St. Anselm. It is not a State Paper. If it were some lying despatch of "the artful Cecil," the learned gentleman would perhaps treat it with more consideration. It is, however, important not only in itself, but as coming after that of Lanfranc, which shows that the peacefulness of Munster was not the mere passing thing which Mr. Froude seems to think a transitory and brief lull in the storm; but a state of affairs which was becoming the usual and recognized condition of the people.

(10) This is one of the strangest fallacies of the modern school of historians who "evolve history out of their own consciousness." We have the clearest proofs that from the days of St. Patrick, Ireland has ever been in relations, the most intimate and loving, with the head of the Catholic Church. It is worthy of remark that whilst every nation in Europe has at some time or other adhered to an anti-pope. Ireland

never made a mistake, but with the instinct of divine faith always clung to the true Pontiff.

(11) Much more proof might be adduced against the authenticity of Adrian's Bull, but what is given suffices. The popular argument now-a-days is that the Pope had no right to give away Ireland, if he gave it, but as Mr. Froude justly remarks, the Pope, 700 years ago, represented the public conscience. The historian admits that 700 years ago there was such a thing as a public conscience, represented by the Pope, in virtue of the agreement and acquiescence of the powers then in existence. Perhaps Mr. Froude would kindly inform us if there be such a thing as a public conscience in existence to-day, and by whom it is represented.

(12) See "The Cromwellian Settlement of Ireland," by John P. Prendergast. The learned author asserts and proves that the design of the English from first to last was to acquire all the land of Ireland into their own hands. Hence arose all the invasions, wars, settlements, plantations, penal laws, etc., which have made Ireland "the Niobe of nations."

(13) Mr. Froude, with more ingenuity than candor, explains this fact by pleading that the dead Irishman and his murderer got Brehon law. Does the learned gentleman forget that the Irishman, John McGilmore, was in the pale, consequently entitled to English law; that he was in the service of an English master, consequently under English law. Reverse the case, and make the Irishman the murderer; would he then get the benefit of Brehon law? Certainly not. Brehon legislation was only recognized when it favored

the English and covered their crimes. The Old Bailey lost an able special pleader when Mr. Froude took to writing history.

(14) Mr. Froude claims for the Geraldines and others of the "old English," that they were "more Irish than the Irish themselves." It is, however, worthy of notice, that in national contests they were not to be trusted, as they generally sympathized with England, and as a rule (not, however, without some exceptions) hated and despised the poor Irish clansmen, who were so faithful to them. It is a fact, that in the rebellion of Thomas, Earl of Kildare, under Henry VIII., the Irish chieftains scarcely interfered at all, having had for once the good sense to let the English king settle it with his feudal Anglo-Norman lords.

(15) For the deplorable want of union amongst the Irish chieftains we have to blame, not only the overweening pride of name and blood, but also the old Celtic constitution, which, however, favorable to freedom, was not calculated to create strong military or united action. It was of old as it is to-day. A free people are not always the strongest, and great military power naturally leans towards despotism.

(16) Mr. Froude is hard upon Shane O'Neil, and with reason, for that chieftain knew how to hold his own. We have it acknowledged, however, by Mr. Froude that Shane was the tanist, and that alone justified the young Prince's action; for the succession was his according to Irish law, and Con O'Neil had no right to change that succession, or that law, without the consent of the people.

(17) The parliament of 1689 did not attaint any landowner for being a Protestant, but simply passed a bill of attainder against every one, Catholic or Protestant, who was in arms against the king, or who refused to obey his proclamation. To designate this as persecution is simply a fallacy.

(18) The churches were desolate and ruined under Elizabeth, simply because the Catholic clergy had to fly, and those who came in their place, came only as plunderers. The Catholic clergy were driven out by the Act of Uniformity, with which their consciences would not permit them to comply; yet Mr. Froude states that the churches were abandoned because Elizabeth would *not* enforce the Act of Uniformity. Strange reasoning!

(19) Mr. Froude asserts that the Earls, O'Neil and O'Donnel fled, because it was discovered that they were plotting again. The history of Ireland tells a different tale, and speaks of a sham plot gotten up to entrap them, fabricated through anonymous letters, and the like agencies. King James, fearing that his reputation might be blemished by the flight of the Earls, issued a proclamation, in which he said, "that it should appear to the world as clear as the sun by evident proof, that the only ground of these Earls' departure, was the private knowledge and inward terror of their own guiltiness." *The proofs thus promised were never produced*, nor is there a shred of evidence of any such conspiracy. In the subsequent plantation of Ulster, the Irish, according to Mr. Froude, were allowed to remain, provided they took the oath of allegiance. Cox, the historian of the time, and others tell

us that the oath demanded of them was the oath of supremacy, very different from that of allegiance. Even then they were allowed to remain only as servants and laborers, holding, by precarious tenure, small portions of the worst and most barren land. The undertakers were strictly forbidden to sell a rood of the land to " the mere Irish." " We found the people," says Edmund Burke, " heretics and idolaters; we have, by way of improving their condition, rendered them slaves and beggars." " They divided the nation," observes the same great statesman, " into two distinct parties, without common interest, sympathy, or connection. One of these bodies was to possess all the franchises, all the property, all the education. The other was to be composed of drawers of water and cutters of turf for them." Mr. Froude chimes in with Hume and others in praising James for his legislation. " Parliament repealed, simply and for ever, every law which had made a distinction between the English and Irish inhabitants of the country." If this salutary law had been made before the Irish were plundered, it would have been better. " After having despoiled an entire sixth-part of the nation of their property, after having dispersed them here and there as suited his purpose, after having transported a large portion of them to the wild wastes of Connaught and Munster, after having impressed into his armies such of them as 'had not cattle or followers of their own,' we are marked with the absurd falsehood that '*he took them under his protection.*' Just such protection as the lawless pirate extends to the peaceful mariners on board an unarmed merchant vessel." (Carey's " Vindiciæ.") It was but poor consolation to the Irish, after one hundred and fifty thousand of them had been robbed and stripped of their property, to make a condescending law abolishing at last the distinction between them and the English. James took good care not to abolish the legal distinction until he had first established the social barrier that divides the rich from the poor.

(20) I do not charge Mr. Froude with defending Strafford's administration. He has two much of the Roundhead spirit in him to do that. He hates Strafford, though he admires worse men. But Strafford's administration fell both under Mr. Froude's notice and mine, and I felt justified in asking the American public, could they approve of it. The impeachment of Strafford for his Irish administration proves no love for Ireland on the part of Mr. Froude's parliamentary friends, but only a hatred of the unfortunate man, for whose blood they were thirsting.

(21) Mr. Froude seems astonished at my account of the massacre at Island Magee. He says Father Burke multiplies the number of the slain by one hundred. According to Mr. Froude there were slain only thirty individuals. According to Leland there were thirty families. According to the author of a "Collection of some of the Massacres and Murders committed on the Irish in Ireland since the 23 October, 1641," appended to Clarendon's "Vindication of the Earl of Ormond," and published in London, in 1662, there were three thousand persons. According to the tradition of the people, which in a matter so comparatively recent must carry some weight, there were three thousand.

Now of all these accounts I hold that the last is most likely to be true. Mr. Froude knows nothing about it and refers us generally to Dr. Reid. Dr. Reid says Mr. Froude proves "how little Leland knew about it." But the author of the collection published his statement within twenty years of the occurrence, appealed to living witnesses, many of them enemies, threw his assertion out before the world and in the teeth of such men as Sir Audley Mervyn, Sir Robert Hanna, and others, who would have contradicted him if they could, and yet his account says Dr. Curry, "has never yet been proved to be otherwise, nor as far as I have learned, even attempted to be proved."

Mr. Froude attempts to establish that Sir Charles Coote's cruelties in Wicklow and elsewhere were merely retaliation for the still greater cruelties of the Irish. I deny it. Sir Charles Coote was rioting in blood before the rising of October, 1641, and I have given sufficient proof that Parsons and Borlase, the Lords Justices, were only too glad of that rising, and too anxious to extend it. As for Mr. Froude's harrowing description from Sir John Temple, it has been exploded before and I need not linger over it. Temple was so much ashamed of his book that he refused to allow a second edition to be published.

# PUBLICATIONS
OF
# P. J. KENEDY,
### Excelsior Catholic Publishing House,
## 5 BARCLAY ST., NEAR BROADWAY, NEW YORK,
*Opposite the Astor House*

| | |
|---|---:|
| *Adventures of Michael Dwyer*........................ | $1 00 |
| *Adelmar the Templar.* A Tale........ | 40 |
| *Ballads, Poems, and Songs of William Collins*........................................ | 1 00 |
| *Blanche.* A Tale from the French................ | 40 |
| *Battle of Ventry Harbor*........................ | 20 |
| *Bibles,* from $2 50 to............................... | 15 00 |
| *Brooks and Hughes Controversy*............... | 75 |
| *Butler's Feasts and Fasts*........................ | 1 25 |
| *Blind Agnese.* A Tale............................ | 50 |
| *Butler's Catechism*................................ | 8 |
| " "  with Mass Prayers............ | 30 |
| *Bible History.* Challoner...................... | 50 |
| *Christian Virtues.* By St. Liguori............ | 1 00 |
| *Christian's Rule of Life.* By St. Liguori........ | 30 |
| *Christmas Night's Entertainments*........... | 60 |
| *Conversion of Ratisbonne*..................... | 50 |
| *Clifton Tracts.* 4 vols......................... | 3 00 |
| *Catholic Offering.* By Bishop Walsh............ | 1 50 |
| *Christian Perfection.* Rodriguez. 3 vols. Only complete edition............................ | 4 00 |
| *Catholic Church in the United States.* By J. G. Shea. Illustrated........................ | 2 00 |
| *Catholic Missions among the Indians*........ | 2 50 |
| *Chateau Lescure.* A Tale..................... | 50 |
| *Conscience;* or, May Brooke. **A Tale**............ | 1 00 |
| *Catholic Hymn-Book*............................ | 15 |
| *Christian Brothers' 1st Book*................. | 13 |

*Catholic Prayer-Books,* 25c., 50c., *up to* . . . . . 12 00

☞ Any of above books sent free by mail on receipt of price. Agents wanted everywhere to sell above books, to whom liberal terms will be given. Address
**P. J. KENEDY,** Excelsior Catholic Publishing House,
*5 Barclay Street, New York.*

| | |
|---|---:|
| *Christian Brothers' 2d Book*................... | $0 25 |
| "         "       3d  "   ................... | 63 |
| "         "       4th "   ................... | 88 |
| *Catholic Primer*........................... | 6 |
| *Catholic School-Book*....................... | 25 |
| *Cannon's Practical Speller*.................. | 25 |
| *Carpenter's Speller*......................... | 25 |
| *Dick Massey.* An Irish Story................ | 1 00 |
| *Doctrine of Miracles Explained*.............. | 1 00 |
| *Doctrinal Catechism*........................ | 50 |
| *Douay*          "     ....................... | 25 |
| *Diploma of Children of Mary*................ | 20 |
| *Erin go Bragh.* (Sentimental Songster.)....... | 25 |
| *El Nuevo Testamento.* (Spanish.)............ | 1 50 |
| *Elevation of the Soul to God*................. | 75 |
| *Epistles and Gospels.* (Goffine.)............. | 2 00 |
| *Eucharistica;* or, Holy Eucharist............. | 1 00 |
| *End of Controversy.* (Milner.).............. | 75 |
| *El Nuevo Catecismo.* (Spanish.)............. | 15 |
| *El Catecismo de la Doctrina Christiana.* (Spanish Catechism)........................ | 15 |
| **El** *Catecismo Ripalda.* (Spanish)............. | 12 |
| **Furniss'** *Tracts for Spiritual Reading*....... | 1 00 |
| *Faugh a Ballagh Comic Songster*............. | 25 |
| *Fifty Reasons*.............................. | 25 |
| *Following* of Christ......................... | 50 |
| *Fashion.* A Tale. 35 Illustrations........... | 50 |
| *Faith and Fancy.* Poems. Savage............ | 75 |
| *Glories of Mary.* (St. Liguori.).............. | 1 25 |
| *Golden Book of Confraternities*.............. | 50 |
| *Grounds of Catholic Doctrine*................ | 25 |
| *Grace's Outlines of History*.................. | 50 |
| *Holy Eucharist*............................. | 1 00 |
| *Hours before the Altar.* Red edges .......... | 50 |
| *History of Ireland.* Moore. 2 vols........... | 5 00 |
| "             "            O'Mahoney's Keating...... | 4 00 |
| *Hay on Miracles* ........................... | 1 00 |
| *Hamiltons.* A Tale.......................... | 50 |
| *History of Modern Europe.* Shea............. | 1 25 |
| *Hours with the Sacred Heart*................. | 50 |
| *Irish National Songster*...................... | 1 00 |
| *Imitation of Christ*.......................... | 40 |

*Catholic Prayer-Books*, 25c., 50c., *up to* . . . . . 12 00

☞ Any of above books sent free by mail on receipt of price. Agents wanted everywhere to sell above books, to whom liberal terms will be given. Address

**P. J. KENEDY**, Excelsior Catholic Publishing House,
*5 Barclay Street, New York.*

**Publications of P. J. Kenedy, 5 Barclay St, N. Y.**

| | |
|---|---:|
| *Irish Fireside Stories, Tales, and Legends.* (Magnificent new book just out.) About 400 pages large 12mo, containing about 40 humorous and pathetic sketches. 12 **fine** full-page Illustrations. *Sold only by subscription.* Only................ | $1 00 |
| *Keeper of the Lazaretto.* A Tale............. | 40 |
| *Kirwan Unmasked.* By Archbishop Hughes..... | 12 |
| *King's Daughters.* An Allegory............... | 75 |
| *Life and Legends of St. Patrick*............ | 1 00 |
| *Life of St. Mary of Egypt*................. | 60 |
| " " *Winefride*......................... | 60 |
| " " *Louis*.... ........................ | 40 |
| " " *Alphonsus M. Liguori*........... | 75 |
| " " *Ignatius Loyola.* 2 vol............ | 3 00 |
| *Life of Blessed Virgin*...................... | 75 |
| *Life of Madame de la Peltrie*................. | 50 |
| *Lily of Israel.* 22 Engravings ............... | 75 |
| *Life Stories of Dying Penitents*............. | 75 |
| *Love of Mary* ............................... | 50 |
| *Love of Christ* ............................. | 50 |
| *Life of Pope Pius IX*....................... | 1 00 |
| *Lenten Manual*.............................. | 50 |
| *Lizzie Maitland.* A Tale...................... | 75 |
| *Little Frank.* A Tale ...................... | 50 |
| *Little Catholic Hymn-Book*................... | 10 |
| *Lyra Catholica* (large Hymn-Book)............ | 75 |
| *Mission and Duties of Young Women*........ | 60 |
| *Maltese Cross.* A Tale....................... | 40 |
| *Manual of Children of Mary*................ | 50 |
| *Mater Admirabilis*........................... | 1 50 |
| *Mysteries of the Incarnation.* (St. Liguori.).... | 75 |
| *Month of November*.......................... | 40 |
| *Month of Sacred Heart of Jesus*.............. | 50 |
| " " *Mary*................................ | 50 |
| *Manual of Controversy*....................... | 75 |
| *Michael Dwyer.* An Irish Story of 1798......... | 1 00 |
| *Milner's End of Controversy*.................. | 75 |
| *May Brooke;* or, Conscience. A Tale........ | 1 00 |
| *New Testament* .............................. | 50 |
| *Oramaika.* An Indian Story................... | 75 |
| *Old Andrew the Weaver*...................... | 50 |
| *Preparation for Death.* St. Liguori........... | 75 |
| *Catholic Prayer-Books,* 25c., 50c., *up to* . . . . . . | 12 00 |

☞ **Any** of above books sent free by mail on receipt of price. Agents wanted everywhere to sell above books, to whom liberal terms will be given. Address

**P. J. KENEDY,** Excelsior Catholic Publishing House,
5 Barclay Street, New York.

| | |
|---|---:|
| *Prayer.* By St. Liguori. | $0 50 |
| *Papist Misrepresented.* | 25 |
| *Poor Man's Catechism.* | 75 |
| *Rosary Book.* 15 Illustrations. | 10 |
| *Rome:* Its Churches, Charities, and Schools. By Rev. Wm. H. Neligan, LL.D. | 1 00 |
| *Rodriguez's Christian Perfection.* 3 vols. Only complete edition. | 4 00 |
| *Rule of Life.* St. Liguori. | 40 |
| *Sure Way; or, Father and Son.* | 25 |
| *Scapular Book.* | 10 |
| *Spirit of St. Liguori.* | 75 |
| *Stations of the Cross.* 14 Illustrations. | 10 |
| *Spiritual Maxims.* (St. Vincent de Paul). | 40 |
| *Saintly Characters.* By Rev. Wm. H. Neligan, LL.D. | 1 00 |
| *Seraphic Staff.* | 25 |
| " *Manual*, 75 cts. to | 3 00 |
| *Sermons of Father Burke,* plain. | 2 00 |
| " " " gilt edges. | 3 00 |
| *Schmid's Exquisite Tales.* 6 vols. | 3 00 |
| *Shipwreck.* A Tale. | 50 |
| *Savage's Poems.* | 2 00 |
| *Sybil:* A Drama. By John Savage. | 75 |
| *Treatise on Sixteen Names of Ireland.* By Rev. J. O'Leary, D.D. | 50 |
| *Two Cottages.* By Lady Fullerton. | 50 |
| *Think Well On't.* Large type. | 40 |
| *Thornberry Abbey.* A Tale. | 50 |
| *Three Eleanors.* A Tale. | 75 |
| *Trip to France.* Rev. J. **Donelan**. | 1 00 |
| *Three Kings of Cologne.* | 30 |
| *Universal Reader.* | 50 |
| *Vision of Old Andrew the Weaver.* | 50 |
| *Visits to the Blessed Sacrament.* | 40 |
| *Willy Reilly.* Paper cover. | 50 |
| *Way of the Cross.* 14 Illustrations. | 5 |
| **Western** *Missions and Missionaries.* | 2 00 |
| *Walker's Dictionary.* | 75 |
| *Young Captives.* A Tale. | 50 |
| *Youth's Director.* | 50 |
| *Young Crusaders.* A Tale. | 50 |
| *Catholic Prayer-Books*, 25c., 50c., *up to* . | 12 00 |

☞ Any of above books sent free by mail on receipt of price. Agents wanted everywhere to sell above books, to whom liberal terms will be given. Address

**P. J. KENEDY,** Excelsior Catholic Publishing House,
5 Barclay Street, New York.

www.ingramcontent.com/pod-product-compliance
Lightning Source LLC
Chambersburg PA
CBHW031741230426
43669CB00007B/437